## A Mary like Me

*a body,*

*O S Lewis*

"Andy Lee voiced the cry of my heart in the first chapter when she wrote about Mary of Bethany: '... her perceived human "flaws" actually become her greatest strengths in the presence of Jesus....' Oh, how different our lives would be if we knew and believed that our flaws don't prevent us from being called! Yes, our humanity confirms our failures, but our confidence in Christ and his power assure our place in his kingdom work. *A Mary like Me* is an engaging, challenging must-read for all women who love Jesus."

— **Vonda Skelton,** founder of Christian Communicators Conference, author, and speaker

"I have had the pleasure and privilege of knowing Andy Lee for many years. I know her heart. I know her passion for God, his Word, and those who love him. I was blessed to read this work in it's infancy, and I remember well how much it moved me, stirring my desire to truly know God, to seek his heart, and to know his will for me. Now I've had the opportunity to read it again. To again be moved. To again feel my spirit soar. *Read this book.* Study it. Grow with it. Find the Mary like you."

— **Eva Marie Everson,** president, Word Weavers International, best-selling, award-winning author and speaker

"Written for women in the midst of all that is life—joy, stress, fear, sadness, blessings, chaos—*A Mary like Me* speaks to your soul. Author Andy Lee captures the essence of what we all feel and channels our emotions back to the One who can help. Her practical application and insight makes this a book to keep for ourselves and give away to those we love. It will always have a place on the shelf where I keep my favorites."

— **Edie Melson,** author of *While My Soldier Serves* and *While My Child Is Away*

"*A Mary like Me* is a gem of a book, one that offers fresh insight into three familiar and beloved women of the Bible. Andy Lee has obviously spent many prayerful hours with these women who, two centuries ago, spent hours and even years in the presence of Jesus. Ms. Lee creatively and intelligently draws biblical truths from their lives—truths that can and will change the lives of believing women today. As you embark on your own Mary Journey, be prepared to learn, to grow, to be challenged, and, most of all, to be blessed."

—**Ann Tatlock,** award-winning novelist and children's book author

"From page one, Andy's insights and scriptural investigation into the three Marys of the Bible left me aching to grab my own Bible and a journal so I could pour out of my heart the lessons God was teaching me. I can't remember the last time a book had this much of a spiritual grip on my soul. Andy takes you on a journey so personal that it makes you feel like you're curled up on the couch next to her. To every woman who has felt that God has called her, this book is for you."

—**Bethany Jett,** author of *The Cinderella Rule: A Young Woman's Guide to Happily Ever*

"If you're anything like me, you will love Andy Lee's *A Mary like Me.* You will love the way she writes. You will love how she handles the Bible. You will love the insights she offers. You will love the 'Marys' you meet. You will love the ways their stories apply to—and change—your story."

—**Bob Hostetler,** author of forty books, including *How to Survive the End of the World* and *The Red Letter Life*

# A Mary like Me

# A Mary like Me

## FLAWED YET CALLED

### ANDY LEE

LEAFWOOD
PUBLISHERS
*an imprint of Abilene Christian University Press*

# A MARY LIKE ME

*Flawed Yet Called*

# LEAFWOOD
## P U B L I S H E R S

*an imprint of Abilene Christian University Press*

Copyright © 2016 by Andy Lee

ISBN 978-0-89112-334-7 | LLCN 2015049765

Printed in the United States of America

Published in association with The Blythe Daniel Agency, Inc., PO Box 64197, Colorado Springs, CO 80962.

LIBRARY OF CONGRESS CATALOGING-IN-PUBLICATION DATA

Names: Lee, Andy, 1966- author.

Title: A Mary like me : flawed yet called / Andy Lee.

Description: Abilene : Leafwood Publishers, 2016.

Identifiers: LCCN 2015049765 | ISBN 9780891123347 (pbk.)

Subjects: LCSH: Christian women--Religious life. | Women in the Bible.

Classification: LCC BV4527 .L44 2015 | DDC 248.8/43--dc23

LC record available at http://lccn.loc.gov/2015049765

Cover design by Thinkpen Design, LLC | Interior text design by Sandy Armstrong, Strong Design

Leafwood Publishers is an imprint of Abilene Christian University Press

ACU Box 29138, Abilene, Texas 79699

1-877-816-4455 | www.leafwoodpublishers.com

16 17 18 19 20 21 / 7 6 5 4 3 2 1

*To Christy Lewis*

1959–2010

*I will see you again.*

# Acknowledgments

A small sign hangs in my kitchen that says, "Faith makes things possible, not easy." I purchased it shortly after I heard God's call to write. It's been a long faith journey filled with twists and turns, ups and downs, and divine acquaintances. But it wasn't my faith or talent that carried *A Mary like Me* to the printing press—it was the faith and expertise of others that brought it to reality, and strengthened my resolve to believe in this project.

I must thank Eva Marie Everson who critiqued my fledgling manuscript. Since that fifteen-minute appointment at my first writers conference, Eva has become a mentor, encourager, editor, and friend. Thank you for taking me under your wing.

Thank you, Ramona Richards, for encouraging me at that conference not to self-publish and to acquire an agent. I held on to your words for years when many friends wanted me to publish this book on my own. Thank you for being his messenger.

Blythe Daniel, thank you for becoming my agent three years after Ramona's advice. Your faith in *A Mary like Me* kept me believing in the book while waiting for the right publisher to come along.

It was a long wait, but the right publisher did find me. Thank you to Leafwood Publishers and the team who championed and polished this work. Special thanks to Gary Myers, acquisition editor, Mary Hardegree, managing editor, and Gene Shelburne, copyeditor. Thank you for your vision, challenges, and expertise.

Finally, thank you to my friends who have encouraged me from the very beginning: Kristin Eitland, Jan Doke, Cathy Hamilton, Jude Jorge, Kim Andrist, and Helen Miller (who will be reading this in heaven with my mom and sister). Thank you to the Wednesday Warriors of Lifepoint Church who were the first *Mary Group*. And thank you to my sweet husband who never doubted for one minute that *A Mary like Me* would be published. I have been humbled by your faith, but please don't quit your job just yet.

And to my Jesus . . . I am your *ebed*. Thank you for this opportunity to serve you. I pray that your love and calling are fulfilled in the lives of those who read this book. "Blessed is she who has believed that the Lord would fulfill his promises to her!" (Luke 1:45). I pray they believe. It's worth every drop of faith.

# Table of Contents

# The Recovery of a Dream

AS I WRITE THESE WORDS, I'M SITTING ON THE SAME BEACH I SAT UPON FIFTEEN YEARS ago in a tidal pool of self-pity. Blessed beyond measure, with a good marriage and two beautiful children, I felt lost. On the North Carolina beach that day as I listened to one of my favorite Christian artists, her words went straight through my headphones to the bottom of my heart. She was singing about dreams.

The tears welled up and gushed out of my eyes as I realized that somewhere between standing at the altar saying "I do" and giving birth to children, I had lost myself in this dream called mommy-hood. I couldn't remember anything I'd ever desired to do beyond rearing a family. So I sat there, feeling terrible about the inability to remember my own dreams, yet feeling selfish and guilty for this sadness. My good friend sat beside me, listening to my woes and confessions as she held my hand and reminded me of the precept I'd shared with her years earlier. She said, "Sing, Andy, sing!"

I knew what she was telling me. She was reminding me to worship the Creator who had formed the very waves rolling toward my feet, and who gave those waters their boundaries. She was reminding me to worship my Savior who had given me hope of everlasting life. She was telling me to take my eyes off the holes in my life and worship the God who alone could fill them with his perfect desires.

So, I sang, even though the singing didn't magically make me feel better. But that *day* of worship has become a *lifetime* of intentional worship and the centrifuge where clarity and vision could rise to the top above the struggles of life.

Please know I don't do this perfectly, and often I need a friendly reminder from my fellow sojourners. But I know that worship was the center from which the dreams I lost in the chaos of life were, in time, resurrected.

One of those dreams is the book you are holding. *A Mary like Me* is tangible evidence that our God truly is the lover of our souls. His grace really is sufficient. He grants us the desires of our hearts as we learn to delight and fall in love with him (Psalm 37:4).

All of us need purpose beyond our own lives. That's why I was so distraught when I couldn't remember any of my own dreams. But as I began to practice thanksgiving and worship in every aspect of life (including changing dirty diapers), I slowly remembered the dreams I held as a young girl.

One of those dreams was to write a book. Thrilled to remember that dream again, I knew I couldn't write just anything. I needed to wait for the topic. I waited fifteen years.

You too may have to wait for the dream to be restored or the assignment to be given, but I encourage you to wait with anticipation. As I waited, God was shaping my personality, and life was writing what would become some of the heart issues of *A Mary like Me.*

God also knew who needed to be in my life to make this book possible. There is no doubt in my mind that he wanted certain people to be a part of this miracle. Just as it takes a village to raise a child, so it takes a community to write a book.

Though a book receives its first breath from the author's soul, and writing demands months of solitude—hours upon hours of silence with only the sound of clicking keys on a laptop—the birth of a book requires friends and family cheering you on. Critique groups help clarify and focus what you're trying to say, prayer warriors intercede, and willing guinea pigs read those first few drafts. I'm so thankful for my village that helped raise this book. I believe there will be a reward for them in heaven.

The rest of my beach story is a tale of God always bringing his children back to a place where we once were lost but now we're found. In the years after my pity party, our military family moved all over the world and then, when my husband retired from the United States Army, we found ourselves back on these sands of North Carolina—a place this Oklahoma girl never imagined would become home. My current house is only ten minutes from the beach I once cried upon. Back on these sands, I sit with a purpose and a passion beyond my dreams. God is creative, faithful, and full of dreams and callings for us that we could never imagine.

Thank you for sharing this book with me. I won't have the privilege of meeting many of you on this side of heaven, but please know I'm praying for you. It's funny, but I feel I know you well even without meeting. How I pray this little book of faith makes a difference for the Kingdom and brings you closer to the One who loves you.

This is my prayer for you as you embark on the *Mary* Journey:

*Oh, Lord, I thank you for the eyes reading these words and the hands holding these pages. Bless them, Lord, with greater revelations of you. Empty their minds of past teachings so they may be able to receive new insight from your living Word. Prepare their hearts, heal their wounds, and open their ears to hear your call. We love you, Lord. We need you. We want to be used by you. Amen.*

# Before We Meet the Marys . . .

IF YOU'VE BEEN GIVEN A DREAM OR HEARD A CALL FROM THE LORD BUT DOUBT THAT HE CAN or will use you, *A Mary like Me* may give you courage to move forward. The Marys of this book were no different from you or me. They were called by God and used by God despite their imperfections. Contrary to tradition, there is no perfect "Mary heart." These Marys were simply women struggling with doubt, fear, and their own human weaknesses, yet they were empowered by a loving God to do what he had called them to do.

Will he do less for us?

Before we look at the lives of these three Marys, we need to address a common problem among women—the comparison game. Whether we admit it or not, we tend to compare ourselves, not only with our modern peers, but also to the women of the Bible. We often consider them perfect before God.

Comparison like this is part of our human nature, but it's dangerous because it's one of the greatest tactics and favorite diversions of the enemy of God. The truth is that someone will always be more talented, more beautiful, or godlier than we are. Always.

But God created each of us to fulfill a special purpose others can't fulfill.

Comparison often stops us from taking those first steps of faith—from painting the picture, writing that song, or publishing our book; we assume it's already been painted or written before. But if God has called *you*; if he has given *you* that dream; then he has purpose that only *you* can fulfill. Someone needs to hear the message only *you* can write or paint. Someone needs to hear the gospel through your lips and shaky voice because you love them and have walked in their shoes.

*A Mary like Me* is written to encourage and help equip you for your specific dream or calling. Helpful features include:

## *Mary Groups*/ Discussion Questions

As you discover your camaraderie with these New Testament women, I encourage you to find a group of friends (or soon-to-be-friends) to discuss the questions for each chapter. As you share your answers, you'll discover that the faith of the other women in your group will encourage you in your faith and help you draw closer to Jesus. Their stories will inspire you. As you share with one another, you will be reminded of the tangible reality and presence of God's love even two thousand years after these first Marys encountered Christ.

Camaraderie with other women is a powerful weapon against the enemy and his lies. Camaraderie kills the power of comparison because it shatters the mirage of perfection. It gives you wings to fly and frees you to be used by God with the personality he's given you. I invite you to register your *Mary Groups* on my website (www.

wordsbyandylee.com), so that others will be able to go to the site and find a group to join in their community or neighborhood.

## Journal Questions

If you hate to journal, I hear your sighs. But let me explain the purpose for the journal opportunities. The prompts provided at the end of each chapter have been written for one purpose: to help create dialogue between you and Jesus. It's so easy to have a prayer life / walk with the Lord that's based only on our petitions and cries. "Monologue" describes the relationship many have with the Lord. The conversation is one-sided.

When you journal prayers and answers, your thoughts sit and breathe. You can write them, read them again, and wait for God's response. You don't have to keep talking because it's in permanent ink on the paper. When we are still and silent, God can speak. Journaling makes us slow down.

My favorite journal is a cheap ninety-nine-cent spiral notebook. Nothing fancy is needed. Just a heart desiring a closer walk with Jesus.

## Appendices

This book will challenge you to set aside some of the conventional beliefs concerning our Marys. As you journey through this new commentary and discover the power of digging into the ancient languages under our English translations, I hope a hunger will stir within you to begin your own research. *Appendix A* further explains my methods of study and the resources I used. *The Key Word Study Bible* (AMG publishers) is one of the most incredible tools I've found for those who want to do more than read the Bible. *Appendix A* will tell you more about this study Bible and other resources available for the non-seminarian.

Through the experience of twenty years of ministry, I've encountered many women suffering with mental illness and depression. The story of Mary Magdalene brings up these topics. *Appendix B* provides armor for such ministry and resources for those who find themselves in the trenches today.

And what kind of teacher would I be if I didn't have some instruction and encouragement for those of you who have been called to lead a *Mary Group*? Whether you are a seasoned leader or a novice stepping out in faith, I hope you'll read *Appendix C* to glimpse the vision for the *Mary Groups* and the essential elements that help make a group grow in faith and intimacy.

## Empowerment

Finally, in order to receive the most God has for you in *A Mary like Me,* be prepared to be honest with yourself, God, and those in your *Mary Group.* God wants to use you for his kingdom with the personality he gave you and the trials you've been through.

You have been called.

He wants to empower you.

That empowerment can only start with a willing *human* heart.

# Chapter One

# Mary of Bethany
## A Defiant Little Sister

MARTHA AND MARY OF BETHANY ARE ALWAYS PRESENT TOGETHER IN SCRIPTURE, BUT IT'S my desire for you to come to know Mary B. alone. With no shadows and no preconceived saintly ideas.

> As Jesus and his disciples were on their way, he came to a village where a woman named Martha opened her home to him. She had a sister called Mary, who sat at the Lord's feet listening to what he said. But Martha was distracted by all the preparations that had to be made. She came to him and asked, "Lord, don't you care that my sister has left me to do the work by myself? Tell her to help me!"
>
> "Martha, Martha," the Lord answered, "you are worried and upset about many things, but only one thing is needed. Mary has chosen what is better, and it will not be taken away from her." (Luke 10:38–42)

I was the baby sister who always got out of doing the dishes. After every Sunday meal at my grandmother's house, the men retired to their favorite recliners to watch the Dallas Cowboys while the women carried dirty plates and half-empty bowls to the kitchen. Conveniently, I always had to go to the bathroom.

For a long time.

I returned just as the last dish was being dried.

Had I lived in the first century, I have no doubt I would have been sitting next to Mary of Bethany, listening to Jesus. But I'm not sure if I would have been sitting there because my heart was pure. I might have had other motives.

Like me, Mary was a little sister. She was also human. Yet her refusal to help her sister Martha with the meal has linked her to a "pure" heart.

Was it really Mary's perfect heart that caused her to ignore her older sister's commands and defy the custom of the day as she sat with the men at Jesus's feet? Or could there be more to the story?

When I tell people I am writing a book, they ask what it's about.

I reply, "Mary of Nazareth, Mary of Bethany, and Mary Magdalene."

It's been interesting to watch their expressions—even Christians who I assume will be familiar with these women. A glazed look comes over some of their faces, confusion colored by embarrassment, because they aren't quite sure who these biblical women were.

Most know Mary Magdalene; her name stands alone, even to the unchurched. Everyone knows Mary of Nazareth as the mother of Jesus, but many need further prompts to place Mary of Bethany

However, the confusion disperses the minute I say, "Mary of Bethany was Martha's sister." This was the clue they needed.

It seems that this Mary lived in the shadow of her big sister her entire life. And despite the recognition Jesus gave her, she is still in the shadow of Martha today. Martha's loud, busy personality can still be heard even two thousand years later—a personality with which many of us identify.

"Mary" was a popular name in biblical times. While I was researching for this book, however, something caught my eye concerning the naming of Mary of Bethany. Keep in mind that I'm a word person, so each little change in words grabs my attention.

Luke introduces us to this Mary when he writes about Jesus visiting her family's home: "As Jesus and his disciples were on their way, he came to a village where a woman *named* Martha opened her home to him. She had a sister *called* Mary, who sat at the Lord's feet listening to what he said" (Luke 10:38–39, emphasis mine). Did you catch the difference in the description of the women's names? Martha is named Martha, but Luke describes Mary's name differently. She is called Mary. I researched several translations to compare the wording. Every translation I read contained this variation in the titles of these two women with the exception of the Holman Christian Standard Bible.

The ancient Greek text also differentiates between these words. Despite the close relationship of these Greek words (*ónoma*, "named," and *kaléō*, "called")[1], I can't assume that Luke trudged to his thesaurus to strengthen the sentence. I think he intentionally employed these specific words. Mary of Bethany was called Mary rather than named Mary. For a reason.

In biblical times, names reflected a person's personality or position in the family. Names were not simply given to distinguish between people as ours are today; they represented the essence of the person—her identity. Martha's name means "lady of the house," "mistress," or "hostess." Her name is the feminine form of *mar*, which means "lord or master."[2] Many commentators believe she was the older, widowed sister of Mary and Lazarus,

Mara-bitter; bitterness is also associated w
  strength; ie a bitter dish described
    as strong.
Ugaritic, Arabic, & Aramaic cognates = bless, strengthen or
                                          commend

and she owned the home. That title explains her actions as she
ran around preparing the meal for their company. Whether or
not she owned the home and was widowed, it is evident that her
identity was wrapped up in hospitality. Almost every scene in the
Bible involving Martha describes her hosting the party. And every
scene demonstrates her "take charge" nature.

Mary's name also assists us as we attempt to imagine her character. The name she was *called* was a Greek word derived from the
Hebrew name, Miryam *(Mir'ih uhm)*. Some mystery hovers over
this name. One source literally wrote, "*miryam—'fat one'?*"[3] (With
a question mark.)

Um . . . that's a terrible name! Surely that source could have
given a better guess. But if that were the meaning of her name,
would it make some of us feel better? Maybe. I've always pictured
all three Marys skinny.

However, when digging for truth, a researcher must find multiple sources to verify her point, and I found no others that agreed
with "fat." But multiple sources gave these meanings: bitter, defiant,
God's gift, and beloved.[4] And the word *rebellion* also appeared in
a few sources.[5] Those may seem an oxymoron rather than words
belonging to one name, and normally, a translator or interpreter
would only choose one meaning that best fits in the context of the
Scripture. However, combining all of these meanings gives Mary
personality. She no longer seems meek and quiet. Boring.

This girl had spunk.

If Luke intentionally described Mary as one *called* rather than
named a bitter, defiant, rebellious, yet beloved, gift of God, Martha's
complaint to Jesus would have been a criticism she typically made
of Mary—the one she and others called defiant.

Imagine this younger sister for a moment. Perhaps she played
the rebellious, defiant, and prone-to-bitterness daughter in their

family. But perhaps, despite these tendencies, Mary was the "beloved" daughter of her daddy.

We all know characters like her, both in real life and in fiction. As I shared this discovery about Mary of Bethany's name with my teenaged daughter, she instantly imagined Mary B. as Elizabeth Bennett of *Pride and Prejudice*, one of her favorite movies. I smile at such a thought. Like this girl called Miryam, Elizabeth Bennett wasn't easily bound by her society's manners.

Mary B. defiantly rebelled against her older sister, the lady of the house, who required Miryam to do the womanly service of the home. Rather than cooking the meal, Miryam sat at the feet of a rabbi as a disciple. This position was only for the men.

Let's step into their home once again and observe this story with consideration of Mary B.'s name, *Miryam*. Imagine the scene:

Jesus was on his way to Jerusalem and needed to stop somewhere for the night. He and his disciples walked through the door of Martha's and Mary's home without "calling ahead," but the Scriptures tell us Martha welcomed them despite their unplanned visit.

It was common in that day for travelers to find food and shelter for the night in homes of strangers. However, Martha's brave outburst to Jesus ordering him to make Mary help her, and Jesus's response to Martha *by name* gives us reason to believe this family and Jesus knew each other well.

John tells us in his Gospel that Jesus loved Mary, Martha, and Lazarus (John 11:5). So, despite (or perhaps because of) their relationship with Jesus, the members of this household had gone into full spin preparing a meal for their beloved guest. However, one member of the household was not concerned with the neatness of the house or with setting the table for dinner or with any of society's dictates.

Perhaps after the initial welcoming of the guests, the disciples and Lazarus sat down to hear Jesus continue his teaching, while the rest of the household prepared the meal. I imagine his words were captivating, awe-inspiring, and Mary B. was mesmerized by both his instruction and his voice. In the presence of Jesus, she forgot who she was and her place in society, so she knelt at his feet with his disciples. As Jesus spoke, she drank in every word like a thirsty plant soaking up rain on a hot summer's day. *This* was where she belonged.

If you've ever felt like you didn't quite fit in with your family or friends, if you've always felt a little different from everyone else, I think you will relate to Mary B. She wasn't the stereotypical daughter of the day. I like her. I want to learn from this girl called a defiant, bitter, rebellious, beloved gift of God.

I would like to challenge you to consider that her perceived human "flaws" actually become her greatest strengths in the presence of Jesus on this famous night. Maybe it wasn't her pure heart that kept her sitting at his feet—not at first. It may have started with defiance that melted into devotion.

Imagine Martha's face, red from the heat in the kitchen and her straggling hair falling from underneath her head covering, as she huffed her way to Jesus. Did she interrupt his teaching when she began to state her case before the Son of God? Did Mary hold her breath as she witnessed her sister's petition for her to join in preparing the meal? Martha was making a scene in front of all of the disciples.

Mary knew her actions were defiant and rebellious, but she'd never known a rabbi like Jesus. He was different. He was the promised Messiah. She wasn't going to do as Martha commanded. Despite her defiance, I wonder if Mary dreaded Jesus's response to her big sister, fearing he would indeed send her back to the kitchen.

If she did fear such a fate, it was for naught. Calmly yet authoritatively, Jesus gave Martha an answer she probably didn't expect. "'Martha, Martha,' the Lord answered, 'you are worried and upset about many things, but only one thing is needed. Mary has chosen what is better, and it will not be taken away from her'" (Luke 10:41–42). Those words must have sounded like music to Mary's ears. She might have let out a sigh and knelt even closer to the Rabbi, gearing up for his next lesson. I don't think she looked with "told you so" eyes at her big sister, but more likely she bowed her head in humble gratitude for the blessing she had received.

Her life would never be the same, and neither would ours. Jesus's recognition of a woman's place in the Kingdom of God as a disciple, learner of his Word, would change the course of the church. That evening Jesus demonstrated the desire of the Father for his daughters, as well as his sons, to be part of the ministry team.

It's difficult for our modern minds to comprehend the enormity of Jesus's actions. We women who go to universities and earn degrees, who vote, run for office, sit in church with our husbands, and in some denominations preach, can't understand why Mary's position at Jesus's feet was such a big deal. To us, it was simply a sweet moment of devotion; but sitting at his feet positioned her with the close groups of male disciples. This wasn't acceptable rabbinical protocol.

The "oral Torah" and women's role in the first-century synagogues paint the position of women at that time. Women couldn't play a significant role in the synagogue because they were unclean during their menstrual cycle. They didn't recite the daily Shema, nor did they read the Torah in the synagogue. They stayed home to farm and make money while their husbands traveled with their rabbi.[6]

We can glean multiple lessons from Scripture. The lesson gathered from this particular story has often been to recognize the importance of sitting at Jesus's feet rather than doing, doing, doing. I don't discount that teaching, and I love the visual of Mary sitting at the feet of Jesus. But perhaps we've missed the significance of Jesus inviting her to sit there.

We traditionally hear Jesus's reply to Martha as, "Mary has chosen the *better*." But there are other ways to translate this answer. The Greek word is *agathos* (ag-ath-os'). It means: good, better, benevolent, profitable, and *useful.*⁷ What if Jesus actually told Martha that Mary had chosen the truly *useful* activity?

In the context of the story, it makes sense. Remember, Martha complained that Mary wasn't helping; she wasn't being *useful*. Martha wasn't asking Jesus to tell her sister to do something *better*. She was demanding that Jesus make her sister *useful* in preparing the meal. Despite her demands, Jesus told Martha that Mary was doing the useful thing.

How could sitting at his feet be useful? Mary's actions were useless and nonbeneficial to Martha, but her actions were useful to Jesus.

Do you see where this is leading us?

A perfect meal may bless us and fill our tummies, but our stomachs will be growling in a few hours. Martha perceived the situation through earthly eyes, but Jesus saw everything with Kingdom perspective. And thus he chose to bless the daughter who defied the accepted customs of the day to learn truth—truth she would one day proclaim to others, thus making her useful for the Kingdom of God.

The King James Version translates this verse with closer accuracy to the word order of the original text. Jesus answered "But one thing is needful: and Mary hath chosen that *good part*, which shall not be taken away from her" (10:42). If you aren't yet convinced of the implications of Jesus's acceptance of women as students of the Torah, disciples of Christ, perhaps the understanding of this Jewish saying will persuade your mind past our traditional teachings. Many of Jesus's phrases are lost on our Western, Christian ears. Jewish context is mandatory, yet very few of us study this way. But God is bringing us around, thanks to wonderful teachers like Ray Vanderlaan, Ann Spangler, and Lois Tverberg. According to Tverberg, Jesus most likely replied to Martha, "Mary has chosen the *good portion*, and it will not be taken away from her." "Good portion" is a phrase often used in the context of learning and knowing the Torah.[8]

There is a time and place for everything; we must be faithful servants of our gifts of the children or homes we have or will be given. However, Jesus changed the course of history for women that night when he not only allowed Mary to sit at his feet as a disciple, but he acknowledged that what she was doing was useful.

Don't we who love Jesus desire to make a difference in this world—to find purpose beyond today—to be useful for the Kingdom?

I've struggled with my own calling of God to preach and teach the Word. No man will ever know the confusion and heartbreak a woman experiences when she believes she's been called to pastor or preach. I've researched, heart searched, and cried out to Jesus for answers concerning women in ministry. Can only men be pastors and preachers?

This question stirs controversy, but Jesus's acceptance of women to join his disciples as students is the model we must remember. It was acceptable and good for Mary to take on this new position.

Words written years later by Paul were personified by Jesus the night he stayed in Bethany. "There is neither Jew nor Greek, slave nor free, male nor female, for you are all one in Christ Jesus" (Gal. 3:26–28).

*Alastair Begg on marriage:*
*Women must choose themselves to place under the authority of a man*

*You are a soul.*
*At resurrection there is no marrying or giving in marriage. They will be like angels. Sexless in eternity!*

*Sexless soul!!*

## a Mary like Me

When Jesus saw Mary B. sitting at his feet with the disciples, he didn't see a woman; he saw her heart—a heart that desired to serve Christ. This is what he sees when he looks at us. We are free to serve, no matter what our gender is. We are also free to serve with the varied personalities he gave us.

Now, I know that women in ministry is a tender subject. And some of you reading may be ready to throw this book away. But I don't want to lose Mary of Bethany in the middle of a church battle. Maybe one day I'll write more on this subject and further explain how I incorporate the Scriptures concerning the silence of women in the church. But, for now, can we simply agree that Jesus wanted Mary to learn about the Kingdom of God so that she could share it with others? There are no oppressive yokes with this interpretation of the Mary and Martha story.

I know so many dear sisters who are the doers in the church. Without their Martha personalities, nothing would get done. I've seen clouds shadow their faces as they translate the meaning of Jesus's words to Martha as an admonition not to focus on the needed tasks at hand. I've seen hurt and confusion in their eyes as they wonder why they were given such personalities.

Scripture should never burden or bring confusion. It may convict, but God's conviction ushers in freedom and healing. If a heavy oppression falls upon you from reading a Scripture or from someone's interpretation, do your research. Study.

This may require digging into the ancient text, the Hebrew or Greek counterparts to our translated words. Appendix A gives resources for such study. Though our Bible is inerrant and inspired by the Holy Spirit, it was written in a very different culture and time, and it has been interpreted by men. We need help understanding what the original authors intended.

God is faithful. I believe he woos us closer to his truth with each generation.

He wants us to wrestle. He desires to give us the blessing.

Jesus told Martha she was upset and worried about many things. I wonder, in context of this Scripture, if Martha was worried not only about the burning pot roast but about her sister's position sitting with the disciples. If this is so, then those of you who identify with Martha's gift of hospitality and service can take off that yoke (another term for "burden") and stand in freedom today as you serve Jesus in the kitchen. Yes, we must kneel at his feet and learn from him, soaking up the truth. But can you now visualize this reprimand from Jesus as a declaration of freedom for women, not an admonishment against Martha's hospitality?

At the same time, those of us who have proudly worn our Mary of Bethany personalities (because we'd rather study our Bible or pray than clean the bathroom) realize her character contained more than a gentle, quiet spirit who liked to listen to Jesus. Her name may prove that Mary's defiance initiated refusal to help Martha—not a perfect heart. Personally, realizing this strips me of any pretentious pride that I once held as I related to Mary of Bethany.

She's more of a kindred spirit than I thought.

Jesus accepted her. Defiance and all. He defended her, despite the name she was *called*. Kudos to our dear Mary (*Miryam*) called defiant, rebellious, bitter, beloved gift of God. May we too be so brave when we find ourselves in the presence of Jesus. In his presence our "worst" qualities can become our best, and we can experience his freedom to be ourselves.

## Journal Opportunity

Be brave enough to sit at the feet of Jesus just as you are—flaws and all. Do you know he gave you that personality? Life might have tweaked it here and there, but the real you down deep—the one that is either loud or quiet, loves a crowd or <u>desperately needs solitude</u>, is <u>quick to place her foot in her mouth</u> or slow to speak—was made <u>by the creator of the universe</u> (Ps. 139:13). List the characteristics you don't like about yourself or the ones that get you in trouble. Write a prayer asking the Lord to employ you on his ministry team and use your "flaws" for his glory.

Angry   Opinionated   Lazy
Selfish   Weak-willed   Self-critical
Others-critical

Lord, I could go on and on with this list. It's so much easier than finding good things about me. Nor can I see how these things can possibly be turned for the good. Please, take my faults, my weaknesses, my failings, and use them for your glory. Because in you the weak are made strong. In weakness your power is perfected and your grace is sufficient. So please perfect your power in weak me.

## Discussion Questions

1. What was the meaning of the name "Mary" which Mary of Bethany was *called*?

   *defiant, rebellious, bitter beloved gift of God*

2. Does this bother you to picture her with these qualities, or does it make you feel as if she is a kindred spirit?

   *It comforts me. No one is perfect, and she was no exception. But God loves her and Jesus commended her.*

3. Have you ever been labeled as rebellious or defiant? If so, how did that affect your view of yourself?

   *Yeah. At the time it just made me more defiant. But later, as I realized my fault, humbled.*

4. Have you been given other labels describing your personality? Do you like them or hate them?

   *Hate them.*

5. Do you agree with the author's interpretation of Jesus's response to Martha?

   *I don't think we can know what He was thinking, but it seems very plausible.*

6. If you have a "Martha" personality, does this interpretation of the Scripture bring freedom?

   *No. I really don't get how it's a release for Martha. It still seems like she chose the lesser pursuit.*

7. How are Mary's character "flaws" changed by Jesus? Is she changed?

   *We have no evidence for how or even if she changed. But surely she must have felt freed by this affirmation. Unless he was simply encouraging her to throw off the stereotyped role & be free.*

33

## Notes

[1] Spiros Zodhiates, ed., *The Complete Word Study Dictionary: New Testament*, (Chattanooga: AMG, 1992), E-Sword iPad edition, Strong's #G3686, #G2564.

[2] Allen C. Myers, ed., *The Eerdmans Bible Dictionary* (Grand Rapids: William B. Eerdmans, 1987), s.v. "Mary."

[3] John A. Lees, "Mary," in *International Standard Bible Encyclopedia*, ed. Geoffrey W. Bromiley (Grand Rapids: William B. Eerdmans, 1986).

[4] *Holman Illustrated Bible Dictionary*, Chad Brand, Charles Draper, and Archie England, eds. (Nashville: Holman Bible Publishers, 2003), s.v. "Mary."

[5] Merrill F. Unger, *New Unger's Bible Dictionary*, R. K. Harrison, ed., new ed. (Chicago: Moody Publishers, 2006), s.v. "Mary."

[6] Lois Tzerberg, "The Reality of Disciples and Rabbis," *Our Rabbi Jesus* (blog), Sept. 16, 2013, http://ourrabbijesus.com/2013/09/16/a-question-about-disciples-rabbis/.

[7] Spiros Zodhiates, ed., *The Hebrew-Original Key Word Study Bible, New American Standard Bible* (Chattanooga: AMG, 1996), s.v. "agathos," 1570.

[8] Lois Tzerberg, "What Was the 'Good Portion' That Mary Chose?" *Our Rabbi Jesus* (blog), Sept. 4, 2012, http://ourrabbijesus.com/articles/what-was-the-good-portion-that-mary-chose/.

# Chapter Two

# Mary of Bethany
## A Bitter Fall

*I heard Jesus was back in town,*
*But I didn't want to go.*
*I was just so confused and hurt when he didn't heal my Lazarus*
*I didn't want my face to show.*

*How could I commune with the One*
*Who could've taken her pain away?*
*Who told me the sickness would not end in death?*
*Who told me she would with us stay?*

*But the truth is, I can't stay away from him.*
*I'm not one for long fights.*
*I'd rather throw in the towel and hear his voice again.*
*I'm tired of the long nights.*

*So today I surrender to the grief.*
*I ask for revelation and life,*
*"Don't let her death be in vain!"*
*May this heartache no longer be strife."*[1]

SHE WAS FUNNY AND SPUNKY, AN ELEMENTARY TEACHER FOR OVER TWENTY YEARS. AT AGE fifty she still had a lot to give to her new grandbaby, her fourth-graders, and her community. But cancer struck a second time, and the diagnosis was grim. When I first learned of this demon's return, I sat in "sackcloth and ashes" in my living room, seeking the Lord's guidance, begging for an extension of my sister's life. I believed God had shown us through Scriptures that she would survive, but that she'd get close to death before healing came. I've never believed anything more strongly. Other believers also received this word for her life, but her healing didn't manifest itself on this side of heaven.

Our biblical Marys were not strangers to the heartache of death and grief. Many who are reading these words know this pain all too well. Death has knocked on my family's door twice within two years. I've experienced the agony of saying good-bye to both my mother and my only sibling.

Unfortunately, death and grief are something no one can escape.

Mary B. faced death and grief also. How did she react to such sorrow? In the last chapter, we left her kneeling at the feet of Jesus, basking in the warmth of being accepted as a disciple. Church tradition has lifted her up to saintly status; we've written books about her perfect heart. But her perfect heart takes a very human turn when she is faced with the death of her brother.

Before I did the research for this book, I envisioned Mary of Bethany as a meek, quiet, dominated little sister of Martha. I no longer see her that way. Now I see her as quiet, yet defiant, with a touch of rebellion. For me, Mary is more likeable *because* of her flaws. These new character developments are the strokes on the painting that bring her to life for me.

Her called name—*Miryam* (bitter, rebellious, defiant, beloved gift of God) becomes even more evident and poignant in our understanding of this new disciple of Christ as we study another section of Scripture.

Let's go to the eleventh chapter of the Gospel of John, where we will meet this dear family in a dire circumstance. Lazarus falls gravely ill. Mary and Martha send word to Jesus requesting his immediate return. Though John tells us Jesus loves this family, the Rabbi and Healer doesn't show up right away. In fact, Jesus tells his disciples that he won't return quickly. Lazarus will die before they reach Bethany.

While Jesus waits to return, Lazarus does die.

Even if you are familiar with this story, read the words of it again, beginning in verse 17:

> On his arrival, Jesus found that Lazarus had already
> been in the tomb for four days. Bethany was less than
> two miles from Jerusalem, and many Jews had come to
> Martha and Mary to comfort them in the loss of their
> brother. When Martha heard that Jesus was coming, she
> went out to meet him, but Mary stayed at home.
>
> "Lord," Martha said to Jesus, "if you had been here,
> my brother would not have died. But I know that even
> now God will give you whatever you ask."
>
> Jesus said to her, "Your brother will rise again."
>
> Martha answered, "I know he will rise again in the
> resurrection at the last day."
>
> Jesus said to her, "I am the resurrection and the life.
> He who believes in me will live, even though he dies;
> and whoever lives and believes in me will never die. Do
> you believe this?"

"Yes, Lord," she told him, "I believe that you are the Christ, the Son of God, who was to come into the world."

And after she had said this, she went back and called her sister Mary aside. "The Teacher is here," she said, "and is asking for you." When Mary heard this, she got up quickly and went to him. Now Jesus had not yet entered the village, but was still at the place where Martha had met him. When the Jews who had been with Mary in the house, comforting her, noticed how quickly she got up and went out, they followed her, supposing she was going to the tomb to mourn there.

When Mary reached the place where Jesus was and saw him, she fell at his feet and said, "Lord, if you had been here, my brother would not have died."

When Jesus saw her weeping, and the Jews who had come along with her also weeping, he was deeply moved in spirit and troubled. "Where have you laid him?" he asked. "Come and see, Lord," they replied.

Jesus wept.

Then the Jews said, "See how he loved him!"

But some of them said, "Could not he who opened the eyes of the blind man have kept this man from dying?"

Jesus, once more deeply moved, came to the tomb. It was a cave with a stone laid across the entrance. "Take away the stone," he said."

"But, Lord," said Martha, the sister of the dead man, "by this time there is a bad odor, for he has been there four days."

Then Jesus said, "Did I not tell you that if you believed, you would see the glory of God?"

So they took away the stone. Then Jesus looked up and said, "Father, I thank you that you have heard me. I knew that you always hear me, but I said this for the benefit of the people standing here, that they may believe that you sent me."

When he had said this, Jesus called in a loud voice, "Lazarus, come out!" The dead man came out; his hands and feet wrapped with strips of linen, and a cloth around his face. Jesus said to them, "Take off the grave clothes and let him go." (John 11:17–44)

Mary and Martha had great faith in *Yeshua*, the Messiah, the Anointed One. He was their friend. They most likely watched Jesus heal strangers, so they certainly had no doubt Jesus would come in haste to heal someone he loved. But, we are told, Jesus didn't respond quickly; he waited two whole days before he started the long journey back to Bethany. When he did return, Lazarus had been dead for four days. Of course, Jesus already knew this would happen. This was God's plan.

I've always thought it interesting that Martha ran to meet Jesus when he neared Bethany, but Mary stayed home. Mary, the one who sat at his feet as a disciple, didn't go to meet him. I don't think it's a stretch to envision her at home, possibly *bitter* toward Jesus (remember, that's one possible meaning of her nickname) for not healing her brother. If any of us have lost a loved one, we can relate to this deep and difficult emotion.

Like me, have you ever found yourself asking Jesus why he didn't come in time to save your relative or friend—why he didn't answer your petition? Mary's absence in Martha's welcoming committee might have been her silent protest to her Rabbi. The rebel sister stayed home to grieve.

But when she did come to Jesus, John tells us that she did so in *haste*.

John records that after Martha and Jesus talked, the older sister went back home, called Mary aside away from the crowd of mourners, and told her, "The Teacher is here, and is asking for you" (11:28). Mary didn't hesitate to run out of the house to find Jesus. She got up and left the house in such haste that the mourners following her assumed she was going to the tomb. If the others presumed she was going to the tomb, I wonder if Mary ran out of the house with great wailing and emotion.

When she reached Jesus, she fell at his feet. This wasn't a simple kneeling gesture or humble bow. The Greek word describing her action is *piptō* (pip-'to).² Two of the definitions of *piptō* are "thrust" and "prostrate." This word describes the falling action of a person overcome with terror or grief. Do these definitions affect your visual image of Mary falling at his feet?

*Piptō* isn't graceful or gentle.

Mary ran to Jesus, flung herself at his feet, and wailed, "Lord! If you had been here, my brother would not have died!" (exclamation marks mine). John continues painting this scene. He tells us: "When Jesus saw her weeping, and the Jews who had come along with her also weeping, he was deeply moved in spirit and troubled" (11:33). Her actions caused Jesus to be distressed and grieved. Take a minute to meditate on this thought. Jesus was troubled. Why would he be troubled when he knew the rest of the story?

What was troubling Jesus was not Lazarus's death.

His sadness was caused by Mary's grief.

When she threw herself onto the ground, she was crying. I don't know why the translators chose the English word "weep" to describe Mary's tears. In our culture, "weeping" arouses the imagery of a quiet and gentle steady stream of tears. But this wasn't Mary's cultural way of mourning.

The Greek text uses the word *klaiō* (klah-yó).[3] This word is the very essence of her tears. Synonyms for *klaiō* are "bewail or moan." Mary's culture mourned with great demonstrations of their pain and sorrow. The grief-stricken sister wasn't just sniffling. She wailed from the depths of her soul.

Can you see her face, pale from lack of sleep, and her eyes swollen from a continual deluge of hot, bitter tears? Mary lay prostrate before the Lord, petitioning an explanation for his inaction. Can you hear her howling as despair took over her voice, and her body crumpled, weary with heartache?

Jesus was moved by her actions. He was distressed by her pain and grief. There aren't very many scenes in the Bible where we are told that Jesus was troubled. We see him frustrated with his disciples many times and agonizing in the Garden of Gethsemane. But Mary's honest, emotional outburst disrupted the peace within him.

It's so hard to grasp the concept of Jesus as both God and man. Scripture makes it clear; he is our high priest, but he also has the ability to empathize with our frail human characteristics. He is able to empathize because he lived in human form and he experienced the sorrow of losing family and friends. This Son of Man is the same life-giving God who will raise his friend Lazarus from the dead.

Despite his privy knowledge, Mary's pain troubled our Jesus. He could have told Mary to calm down because it would soon be okay. He could have told her she was overreacting. But rather than rebuke her emotional outburst, he cried with her and the other mourners surrounding them. This is our Jesus. Despite his foreknowledge of the future, he is *in the moment* with us.

I've found myself in Mary's shoes. I've petitioned and petitioned. I've cried and wailed to Jesus to come and heal my mother

41

and my sister. Jesus is my friend. I have great faith in him. I know he can heal the sick, give sight to the blind, and hearing to the deaf. And, I believe he can restore a sixty-year-old whose mind is lost to Alzheimer's or a body with stage four lung cancer.

But despite my petitions for their healing, my mother and my sister declined every day.

Please know I have been *piptō* before the Lord, anointing my carpet with uncontrollable tears. I've been so bold as to remind him at the top of my lungs that he is a faithful God, and he must prove himself true to my loved ones even if he wouldn't heal them.

Those prayers, he answered.

The Lord was faithful to my mom. The nursing home was brand new, run by a church, and built specifically for Alzheimer's patients. She was not only loved by her family but also by the nursing staff on her floor. That fact alone was an answer to one of my prayers.

Her smile lit up the room, and everyone loved her laugh, even when she could no longer speak. After eight years of waiting for Jesus to show up, and grieving the loss of my mother because Alzheimer's takes its victims before they are actually gone, the Lord came and called her out of her tomb. The graveclothes of Alzheimer's and Parkinson's were taken off, and I knew she was free.

Mom's dying brought some relief, but my sister's death knocked me off my faith horse. I really believed Jesus would come heal *this* Lazarus. He didn't, at least not as I preferred.

Still, Jesus's tender interaction with the grief-stricken Mary brought great comfort during a long season of grieving.

I've been touched by the empathy of Jesus, the Creator-man of the world, the Resurrection himself, who cried with Mary. He didn't tell her that it was good for Lazarus to be dead. Or that he was in a better place. Or that "one day all this will make sense."

He cried with her.

I've been praying for a friend who just lost a loved one. Along with peace and comfort, I've petitioned God that she might feel God's permission to grieve. It may sound like a silly prayer, but in my own experience of grief, I felt as if I wasn't supposed to mourn because of the hope of heaven. Because of the different emotions running through my soul, I felt that I was a weak Christian. None of those emotions even remotely resembled joy.

Somewhere in our Puritan-American background, we lost the permission to grieve with demonstrative emotion. We hold our breath and restrain the wails begging to be released from our chests. I stood in this uncomfortable position at my sister's viewing. How I wished at that moment to be from another culture. A culture that grieved out loud and together. I struggled with those religious condolences reminding me of our faith in heaven. Those words brought comfort when Mom died but no relief after my sister's death. Perhaps they brought comfort because Mom had already been gone for so long. But when offered to me regarding my sister, they only served to make me angry.

The sadness I experienced after Christy's death sank to my toes. I've never known such depths of grief. But during those first few weeks, the Lord reminded me of these four important truths:

1. He created us as relational beings.
2. He gave us the capacity to love.
3. It was his divine design for us to desire companionship, family, and relationships.
4. Relationship is who he is.

So when we lose someone, despite our promise of heaven and eternity together, we grieve because we miss them. It's that simple. God knows our hearts. He understands our loss, and he will not leave us in the grief. He doesn't want us to stay there, but he does understand. Nothing demonstrates this better than his reaction to Mary's grief. He cried with her. He cries with us.

I don't believe Jesus is rejoicing in heaven when another disciple comes home—not yet. The angels may be rejoicing, but I believe Jesus cries with those still on this earth. The ultimate rejoicing will come when all is made new, when heaven and earth are restored, our bodies are resurrected, and we reign and rule with Jesus together. Until then, we have permission to grieve.

Some who are reading these words may be holding back the grief, anger, and questions you have for Jesus. You have been taught that to let them out would be disrespectful to your Lord or to your faith. Don't believe that. Don't hold them in anymore. Wail before the Lord as our *bitter* Mary did. Thrust yourself before his feet, and cry out to the only one who can empathize with you entirely. He knows your heart's desires and pain.

Don't miss Mary's position before the Lord; she wailed to him as she *lay at his feet*. Mary's honest, humble response to Jesus created a much different response from Jesus than Martha's, in spite of their having said the exact same words to him. I don't mean to suggest that Martha's response wasn't honest, but it was spoken differently than Mary's. I believe there is power when we are humbly prostrate before the Lord. Broken. *Piptō* before him with all of your honest emotions.

If you've struggled with grief and are unsure of your loved one's relationship with the Lord and secured salvation, let me encourage you with this: we are promised that "the Lord is . . . not wanting anyone to perish, but everyone to come to repentance" (2 Pet. 3:9). He is a holy God of judgment, but he is also a God of understanding and empathy, and he is a God of many chances. In his relationship with his chosen people, the Israelites, he has demonstrated his faithfulness time and again, and he has demonstrated his faithfulness to the Gentiles by sending Jesus to die for us all.

A good friend of mine put this pain of not being certain of a loved one's salvation in a wonderful perspective. One day, as she sat at my kitchen table, she described an insight from the Lord she received while begging for her mother to survive a gunshot wound to her head.

Her mother was not a Christian. She had denied the Lord many times, yet as my friend desperately prayed for her to survive, the Lord showed her the many times in her mother's life when he had been faithful to give her opportunities to know him.

At that moment Katherine was able to release her mother to life or to death, to heaven or to hell. Despite her mother's salvation or lack thereof, she knew God himself wouldn't judge her mother unfairly. Her ability to find peace on that horrendous day and the grace to release her mother were granted because her focus was not on her mother and the situation. Her focus had shifted to the goodness and faithfulness of God.

God knows the hearts and minds of our loved ones better than we do. He alone knows what happens in the last minutes of life. We must trust his goodness and his faithfulness. Her mother didn't die on the operating table that day but lived to proclaim her faith in Christ. My friend's Lazarus was given a second chance.

Another friend told me of a dream after her stepfather's death. She didn't have a good relationship with this alcoholic, abusive man. She hated him. At his funeral she didn't even consider his chance to be in heaven because of the vile man she knew him to be. But the night after the funeral, she dreamed that her stepfather was sitting next to Jesus. Kathy didn't hear Jesus's words, but she knew her stepfather was being given the opportunity to choose heaven or hell. Her dream ended and she woke up knowing the grace of our God. His grace extends even to the greatest of sinners. Through the dream, his grace also released her hardened heart.

As you read this chapter, if you find yourself muddy in the furrows of prayer, lifting up guttural petitions for someone you love, or if you find yourself deep in the despair of grief, I pray these words bring you comfort and a touch of soul healing. Jesus loves you and the one you would give your life to see healed on this earth. He loves you, he grieves with you, and he has a better plan.

As I cling to the story of Mary and Martha and Lazarus in my grief, I cling to the twenty-first chapter of Revelation and the promises John penned from his vision of a new Kingdom.

> Then I saw "a new heaven and a new earth," for the first heaven and the first earth had passed away, and there was no longer any sea. I saw the Holy City, the New Jerusalem, coming down out of heaven from God, prepared as a bride beautifully dressed for her husband. And I heard a loud voice from the throne saying, "Look! God's dwelling place is now among the people, and he will dwell with them. They will be his people, and God himself will be with them and be their God. 'He will wipe every tear from their eyes. There will be no more death' or mourning or crying or pain, for the old order of things has passed away." (Rev. 21:1–4 NIV)

He will wipe away our tears.

What kind of God would care enough to take the time to gently touch my face and wipe my tears rather than just handing me a tissue? He is a compassionate, feeling God, but his love doesn't get in the way of his purpose. He plans to bring us home. He has promised to take us to live where there will be no more death, no more mourning, no more crying, and no more pain. There will be no graveclothes or funeral clothes in heaven.

I'm so thankful that we have a Savior who loves us, mourns with us, and knows our deep sadness of soul. Believing the sovereign God cares for us through such sorrow is paramount to this human who longs to be understood by her Creator. His love for me softens the pain as I continue to grieve the loss of my mom and sister. But my gratitude for his compassion doesn't compare to my thankfulness that, as he called Lazarus out of a physical grave, Jesus also calls us out of a spiritual grave.

Jesus loves you. Your pain troubles him as Mary of Bethany's did. Let his tender heart heal yours today, and trust the Resurrection himself, who has the power and desire to set your loved one and mine free. Would you pray with me?

You have searched me, LORD,
and you know me.
You know when I sit and when I rise;
you perceive my thoughts from afar.
You discern my going out and my lying down;
you are familiar with all my ways.
Before a word is on my tongue
you, LORD, know it completely.[4]

---

So I give you my bitterness and pain today.
You know it already.
Here it is.
Here I am.
Please restore my hope and my heart as you did Mary's.
Amen.[5]

## Journal Opportunity _____

If you feel betrayed by your friend Jesus and are struggling with the death or sickness of a loved one, journal those honest feelings to him. After you've written the prayer, all alone before your God, fall before his feet and let him hear your cries. He loves you. He has a plan.

## Discussion Questions

1. What are the definitions of the words *klaiō* and *piptō*? Do these words change your visual image of this scene?

   *Klaiō - be wail or moan*
   *Piptō - thrust, prostrate*
   *No.*

2. It could be assumed that Mary felt betrayed by Jesus. Have you ever felt betrayed by him? When?   *Key word!*

   *Yes. when I don't see myself changing. when I fail to meet my expectations by what a Christian ought to be or do.*

3. Have you been honest with God with these emotions or have you felt it would be wrong to voice your anger to Jesus?

   *Mostly honest, yet sometimes, perhaps, feeling guilty over it,*

4. How did Jesus react to Mary's honest outburst?

   *With empathy.*

5. What is your favorite part of this Scripture?

   *Jesus empathy.*

## Notes

[1] Poem written by author after her sister's death.

[2] "Lexicon :: Strong's G4098 - *piptō*," Blue Letter Bible: NIV, accessed February 3, 2015, http://www.blueletterbible.org/lang/lexicon/lexicon.cfm?Strongs=G4098&t=NIV.

[3] "Lexicon :: Strong's G2799 - *klaiō*," Blue Letter Bible: NIV, accessed February 3, 2015, http://www.blueletterbible.org/lang/lexicon/lexicon.cfm?Strongs=G2799&t=NIV.

[4] Psalm 139:1–4.

[5] Author's prayer.

# Chapter Three

# *Mary of Bethany*
## Prophetic Anointing

AVE YOU NOTICED THAT EVERY TIME WE SEE MARY OF BETHANY, SHE IS SOMEWHERE NEAR the feet of Jesus? We've seen her sitting at his feet as a disciple, and we just witnessed her lying prostrate before him in a puddle of grief.

Now we will watch her bow so lowly on her knees that she can wipe Jesus's feet with her hair. Her face brushes against the feet of the Savior as she anoints him with the most extravagant gift she can give.

Imagine how low you'd have to get to dry someone's feet with your hair. Face near the ground is where we find Mary B. in one of the most beautiful acts of worship in the Bible—performed by the girl called defiant, rebellious, bitter, beloved, child of God. I think *Miryam* had to be all of these things to do what she did at this dinner party. Let's read the Scripture:

Six days before the Passover, Jesus arrived at Bethany, where Lazarus lived, whom Jesus had raised from the dead. Here a dinner was given in Jesus' honor. Martha served, while Lazarus was among those reclining at the table with him. Then Mary took about a pint of pure nard, an expensive perfume; she poured it on Jesus' feet and wiped his feet with her hair. And the house was filled with the fragrance of the perfume. But one of his disciples, Judas Iscariot, who was later to betray him, objected, "Why wasn't this perfume sold and the money given to the poor? It was worth a year's wages." He didn't say this because he cared about the poor but because he was a thief; as keeper of the money bag, he used to help himself to what was put into it. "Leave her alone," Jesus replied. "[It was intended] that she should save this perfume for the day of my burial. You will always have the poor among you, but you will not always have me." (John 12:1–8)

Use your imagination to experience this scene. Picture Jesus reclining on pillows, legs bent at an angle behind him, his body propped on one elbow, his other hand free for eating and drinking. Lazarus reclined at the table with Jesus and his disciples, while Martha served.

She was still serving. Don't you love it? It was what gave her pleasure and purpose. There is no indication during this meal that Martha was annoyed with Mary, who also was doing her own thing, the thing that gave her pleasure and purpose. Nor is there any indication that Jesus scolded Martha for cooking. They were free to be themselves with the Rabbi.

The aroma of unleavened bread and roasted lamb filled the room as Martha dished up the food. They were celebrating the new life Lazarus received from Christ just a short time before. This meal was a great celebration of life, with music playing, wine flowing, and laughter filling the home. At least it was until Mary brought her gift to her Rabbi, the man she and her family recognized as Yeshua Messiah.

Perhaps she entered the room with eyes facing the floor. Her hands cautiously carried the most valuable article from her dowry. No one noticed she had walked in until she began to pour the perfumed oil over the feet of Jesus. The smell of the oil was strong, and its intoxicating fragrance drew attention to the one pouring out her gift.

All eyes fell upon Mary.

John writes: "Then Mary took about a pint of pure nard, an expensive perfume; she poured it on Jesus's feet and wiped his feet with her hair. And the house was filled with the fragrance of the perfume" (12:3).

Oh, how slowly and carefully Mary poured that oil as she gently anointed Jesus. Her head was most likely uncovered as her hair fell on Jesus's feet, and she wiped them with great care. John didn't mention tears, but I do imagine Mary crying as she prepared Yeshua for burial.

Though we assume that Mary anointed Jesus out of a grateful heart for the restored life of her brother, there was much more in her heart than thankfulness; she was performing this beautiful demonstration of love in preparation for Jesus's death.

It was Jesus who informed the gaping crowd of her purpose. Jesus justified her gift. "[It was intended] that she save this perfume for the day of my burial" (John 12:7).

Her perfume wouldn't be used on the night of her wedding nor for a gift to the poor.

Her gift was for Jesus.

The Messiah defended her actions when immediate accusations and disapproval came from Judas and other dinner guests. I love how Jesus protected Mary. This is the second time he came to her defense. First with her sister, this time from one of his own disciples. One of the Twelve. And, just as he'd done previously, Jesus rebuked Mary's antagonistic naysayer. He said to Judas, "Leave her alone" (Mark 14:6).

Our three English words are employed to translate the single word admonition, *aphiēmi* (af-ee-ay-mee). The definitions I found for this Greek word were: "Don't send away" or "Don't dismiss."[1] You could argue that "leave her alone" implies the same translation, but I believe "don't send her away" indicates that Jesus isn't merely protecting her from the bullies; he is recognizing the importance of her presence in the room. Just as he recognized the value of her presence at his feet as a disciple just a few pages ago.

If Mary's presence was valued by Jesus, I believe our presence is also.

Does this speak to your soul? What would it mean to have Jesus recognize and defend your attendance in a room? The same Jesus who recognized the value of Mary's company recognizes ours. I pray that you believe this truth.

Jesus doesn't tolerate our presence; he didn't just tolerate Mary of Bethany. He desired for her to be there, and he acknowledged her gift as one of significance. He is the same Savior today as he was that night in Bethany. And we are no different from the defiant, rebellious, bitter, beloved gift of God *called* Mary.

I'm also blessed by Jesus's defense of Mary of Bethany because it demonstrates God as our protector. He is our shelter, our stronghold of safety. The men who wrote the psalms also knew God as their refuge and strength and acknowledged those attributes. Listen to these words believed to be penned by Moses:

He who dwells in the shelter of the Most High
   will rest in the shadow of the Almighty.
I will say of the LORD, "He is my refuge and my fortress,
   my God, in whom I trust."
Surely he will save you from the fowler's snare
   and from the deadly pestilence.
He will cover you with his feathers,
   and under his wings you will find refuge;
   his faithfulness will be your shield and rampart.
   (Ps. 91:1–4)

How we need a Savior who will be our shield and rampart when the naysayers, whether voices from actual flesh and blood or voices in our own heads, taunt us and disapprove of our offering to the Lord.

Can you picture Jesus rising up to Mary's defense? Do you see the shield of the Lord around her once again? Her encounter with the living Christ joined her with another psalmist when he wrote: "But as for me, it is good to be near God. I have made the Sovereign LORD my refuge" (73:28).

Mary always placed herself near Jesus.

But Jesus did even more than protect Mary and recognize the importance of her presence. The Gospels of Matthew and Mark record very similar accounts, but Jesus's response in these two Gospels further proves his appreciation of Mary and the importance of her actions. I love what Jesus says according to Mark:

"Leave her alone [don't dismiss her]," said Jesus, "Why
are you bothering her? She has done a *beautiful* thing
to me. The poor you will always have with you, and
you can help them at any time you want. But you
will not always have me. She did what she could. She
poured perfume on my body beforehand to prepare for

my burial. I tell you the truth, wherever the gospel is preached throughout the world, *what she has done will also be told, in memory of her.*" (14:6–9, addition and emphasis mine)

This is my Jesus.

Your Jesus.

Mary's Jesus.

He not only protected Mary of Bethany and acknowledged the value of her presence, but he also called her offering beautiful. To the others around the table, Mary's offering was offensive and bothersome, but to Jesus her offering was lovely.

Why was it so beautiful to Jesus? Because the Savior, the Creator of the universe, who knit Mary (and you and me) together in our mothers' wombs,[2] always sees the heart of the giver. He knew Mary's gift was given with a heart of thankfulness and recognition of his deity. Whether or not Mary understood the significance of her obedient actions, Jesus did.

Do you need to know that you and your offerings poured out to Jesus are beautiful to him? When our gifts are given from a heart of faith and love, as Mary's were, they are beautiful to Jesus. Her offering is one that might seem morbid or faithless because it involved preparation for death, but Jesus looked right past the present and acknowledged her service as one that will never be forgotten.

It hasn't been forgotten. Matthew and Mark don't give the anointer a name, but John specifically tells us that Mary was the one who anointed Jesus. He tells us twice, as if he greatly wanted the readers to know Mary B. was the person who anointed the Christ: this Mary, whose brother Lazarus had lain sick, was the same one who poured perfume on the Lord and wiped his feet with her hair. Then Mary took about a pint of pure nard, an expensive perfume; she poured it on his feet and wiped his feet with her hair (John 11:2, 12:3).

Commentators theorize that because Matthew's and Mark's Gospels were written during a period of great persecution for believers, the Gospel writers left out Mary's name to protect her. But they didn't leave out the names of Lazarus and Martha. Why would this be?

Mary's actions were socially unacceptable and dangerously demonstrative of her faith in Jesus as God's Son. F. B Meyer writes, "The earlier Gospels (Matthew 26; Mark 14) do not mention Mary's name, probably because the whole family might have suffered for their intimate identification with Jesus. But when this Gospel (John) was written, the beloved trio had been gathered home to God."[3]

Mary of Bethany dared to demonstrate total vulnerability and worship a man the religious authorities believed to be only a prophet or less. It was courageous worship.

Not only was this worship bold, it was disgraceful. There is no mention of either sibling's thoughts on Mary's latest faux pas. Did Lazarus hold his tongue this time? I wonder if Mary feared angering her only brother as she "wasted" a whole year's worth of wages. What would replace this precious item, most likely from her dowry?

Did Mary B. fear dishonoring her family as she let her hair down to dry Jesus's feet? A woman's hair was precious. Modest women kept this treasure covered. Her actions should have only been carried out behind closed marital doors. Yet she unashamedly came to Jesus as a bride to her bridegroom. The Bridegroom is Christ.

What urged Mary to perform this specific act? Had the Holy Spirit filled her with overflowing love as well as premature grief—grief much like the pain she felt when Lazarus died? Intense pain she would experience at the death of Jesus only a few days from this very night. Was she making a scene?

Yes.

Mary's actions exhibited great faith. She denied her own hope for an earthly Messiah, followed the Spirit's leading, and did the unthinkable. She prepared Jesus's body for burial before his actual death.

We've seen that Mary of Bethany wasn't always obedient. Anointing Jesus out of a thankful heart for her brother's life would have been effortless for her, but I wonder if she held reservations about anointing the Lord for the purpose of burial. Did she try to second-guess herself, hoping that if she didn't perform this duty, his death would be postponed? If she did, the urging of the Spirit must have been too strong to deny.

Whether or not she understood the significance of her actions, she followed the leading of the Holy Spirit.

One of my dearest friends is a seventy-five-year-old saint from the mountains of North Carolina. Her family calls her Granny. She is a spunky, shiny, classy woman of God. I love to hear her stories of the Spirit's promptings in her life.

As our *Mary Group* discussed this chapter, she shared with us a moment when the Lord led her to do something out of her comfort zone. It involved a man, a pan of water, and the Spirit's leading to wash this Bible study leader's feet.

Her eyes lit up with love for the Lord as Granny told us her story. She explained to our *Mary Group* that God had prompted her a few days before the Bible study to wash her leader's feet at the next meeting. Granny confessed to us her trepidation to perform this task, but her fear didn't stop her.

"God strengthened and blessed me with each step as I followed his leading," she continued, "As I washed his feet, the entire room fell silent, and the presence of Jesus filled the place."

Her words painted the scene of people enveloped in the heavy glory of God.

I wish I could have been there.

Have you been prompted by the Holy Spirit to do something for someone? It's one thing to have the vision of an angel before you proclaiming your destiny, as Mary of Nazareth did, but the Holy Spirit isn't so easy to see. Do you recognize his promptings?

Pray for ears to hear his voice and faith to follow through. Remember, Mary of Bethany, *Miryam*, was a disciple of Jesus; she listened to his words and studied his teaching as closely as she could. She knew her Rabbi.

As we come to know him, we become more assured of the promptings of his Spirit.

Mary was honest with Jesus. She prostrated herself before him and wailed her questions when Lazarus died. Her humble honesty with the Savior prepared her to receive the Holy Spirit's guidance. Judas couldn't receive it, but Mary of Bethany had nothing to hide. When we know Jesus and we have given him all of our soul, hiding nothing, we'll easily distinguish his voice from our own.

Even after years of loving and serving the Lord, I still find myself in cycles doubting my ability to hear and have assurance of the Spirit's promptings. I'm learning that when the Lord seems silent, I need to ask him to reveal if I've stepped out of his will. When I stop beating around the bush and obey what he has been prompting me to do (but I have been too faithless or defiant to do it), I find the fruit of joy and peace in my life.

Until I obey, I am fearful, anxious, and discouraged.

The Lord will continue putting something in front of me to make his will obvious. He never gives me the full motion picture from start to ending; he only lights the one step of the path I must take, for that moment, as I trust his leading.

Unfortunately, many of us know all too well what it's like to refuse a prompting, only to wish later that we could go back in time to comply with the Spirit's leading. Listen to this story from a dear sister:

> When my father was in the hospital, I took care of him. After a week, I was relieved by my niece so I could go to a speaking event. I gave Daddy a hug, told him I loved him, and then wheeled my luggage out of the room. The Holy Spirit whispered, *You will never see your father alive again. Go back and hug him one more time.* My logic said, "But if you do, then you are saying you believe you won't see him again. So, if you don't, then he won't die." There was every reason for Daddy to live; no reason for him to die—except what God had told me. I kept walking . . . and Daddy died. I never saw him alive again. That has absolutely tortured me over the years. Why had I thought I could trick God into keeping my father alive?

Perhaps Mary also had to trust the Spirit's promptings and deny her logic as she took one step, then another, into the dining room filled with men reclining around the table on this unforgettable night. Whether or not she struggled with the Spirit's promptings, she finished what she intended to do.

With each drop of oil upon Jesus's feet and each sweep of her hair and face touching God-wrapped-in-skin, with each step of obedience, she was filled to overflowing by the Spirit himself. In that prophetic moment, she saw no one else in the room but Jesus.

## Journal Opportunity

What would be an act of extravagant worship for you? Write a prayer asking the Lord to open your ears to his promptings, to grant you greater courage and freedom in worship, and to strengthen your assurance of his leading.

Lord, I want to serve you. Wholeheartedly, unreservedly. But I am reluctant and selfish. Please give me ears to hear your voice, and a heart to follow you, and confidence in my discernment of your voice.

## Discussion Questions

1. What does the original word *aphiēmi* mean?

   *Don't send away.*

2. How does the translation of John 12:7 in your Bible differ from this Greek word?

   *Let her alone.*

3. Is it significant to you that Jesus would say, "Don't send her away?" What does this mean to you?

   *He wants her there, to do what she was called to do, what she was meaning.*

4. Do you believe that your presence is important to Jesus? Why or why not?

   *In my head, yes. In my heart no, because I find myself worthless.*

5. What do you think prompted Mary to perform this daring demonstration of worship? *Love for Jesus.*

6. Have you ever felt prompted by the Spirit to do something out of your comfort zone? If so, what was it? How did it turn out?

7. Have you ever received a prompting from the Spirit but denied it? What happened?

   *Yes. Grandma's death. I didn't get to see her.*

## Notes

[1]Spiros Zodhiates, ed., *The Hebrew-Original Key Word Study Bible, New American Standard Bible* (Chattanooga: AMG, 1996), 1596.

[2]Psalm 139:13.

[3]F. B. Meyer, *The Bethany Parallel Commentary on the New Testament* (Minneapolis: Bethany House, 1983), 604.

# Chapter Four

# *A Nameless "Mary"*

## A Kindred Spirit

I BECAME OBSESSED WITH ONE TASK AS I RESEARCHED MARY OF BETHANY'S CHARACTER. I wanted to prove that all four Gospel accounts of a woman anointing Jesus at a dinner could be one and the same despite discrepancies. Actually, I really wanted to prove that the "sinful" woman in Luke's Gospel who anointed Jesus was our one and only Mary of Bethany.

Mary B. has become a kindred spirit. We have discovered that she wasn't the sterile, perfect, always obedient woman tradition has painted. We now can picture her as a spunky, passionate, and sinful woman. Did you cringe when you read the word "sinful"? I did when I wrote it. But we've seen that Mary did have a rebellious side. She wasn't perfect; just like we aren't. She was human.

We are sinful. Sin comes in all shapes and sizes. Though we know all sin separates us from the presence of God, we rate particular sins worse than others. After desperately trying to link Luke's anointer with Mary of Bethany, I've come to the conclusion that it is indeed the sin of Luke's heroine that separates these two women.

I'd like to walk you through the process that led me to this decision. We will find that, even though these heroines who anoint Jesus are two very different women, they are kindred spirits linked by love for Christ. It's this love that unites their offering—not their sin nor their DNA.

Read Luke's account:

> Now one of the Pharisees invited Jesus to have dinner with him, so he went to the Pharisee's house and reclined at the table. When a woman who had lived a sinful life in that town learned that Jesus was eating at the Pharisee's house, she brought an alabaster jar of perfume, and as she stood behind him at his feet weeping, she began to wet his feet with her tears. Then she wiped them with her hair, kissed them and poured perfume on them.
>
> When the Pharisee who had invited him saw this, he said to himself, "If this man were a prophet, he would know who is touching him and what kind of woman she is—that she is a sinner."
>
> Jesus answered him, "Simon, I have something to tell you."
>
> "Tell me, teacher," he said.
>
> "Two men owed money to a certain moneylender. One owed him five hundred denarii, and the other fifty. Neither of them had the money to pay him back, so he canceled the debts of both. Now which of them will love him more?"

Simon replied, "I suppose the one who had the bigger debt canceled."

"You have judged correctly," Jesus said.

Then he turned toward the woman and said to Simon, "Do you see this woman? I came into your house. You did not give me any water for my feet, but she wet my feet with her tears and wiped them with her hair. You didn't give me a kiss, but this woman, from the time I entered, has not stopped kissing my feet. You didn't put oil on my head, but she has poured perfume on my feet. Therefore, I tell you, her many sins have been forgiven—for she loved much. But he who has been forgiven little loves little."

Then Jesus said to her, "Your sins are forgiven."

The other guests began to say among themselves, "Who is this who even forgives sins?"

Jesus said to the woman, "Your faith has saved you; go in peace." (Luke 7:36–50)

The New Living Translation subheads this passage, *Jesus Anointed by a Sinful Woman*. I found other Bible versions that refer to her as a "sinful woman," even though a glance through this Scripture doesn't reveal her sin. The connotations of the Pharisee's thoughts have linked this woman to prostitution.

I wrestled with this as I tried to turn this woman into Mary B. Is there evidence of this woman's sinful vocation? As I dug deep into the text, I found no indication in the Greek text of prostitution. So, I had decided that the subtitle of this passage of Scripture was misleading, until I studied the words of the Pharisee's thoughts, "If this man were a prophet, he would know who is *touching* him and *what kind* of woman she is—that she is a *sinner*" (7:39, emphasis mine).

I researched three words trying to prove my point or to agree with tradition. Two had no revelatory meanings. The word *sinner* in the Greek simply means "missing the mark." Likewise, "*what kind of woman*" can be a reference to her home country or her religion; it doesn't describe her profession. These words didn't shade the sentence with any colors of prostitution; therefore I was preparing myself to believe that she *could be* Mary of Bethany. I thought the Pharisee and the Bible editors had judged this woman unfairly, just as we "judge books by their covers."

However, when I looked up the word *touching* in the Greek, I discovered the culprit that implied the woman's occupation. Remember, the Pharisee thought, "If this man were a prophet, he would know who is touching him." The Greek word for "touching" is *haptō* (hap-'tō). The definition of this word is very interesting. It is distinguished from the word *psēlaphaō* (psay-laf-'ah-o) which means simply to touch the surface of something. *Haptō* is defined as: *Such handling of an object as to exert a modifying influence upon it or upon oneself, manipulating . . . figuratively, it is a euphemism for excessive sexual intimacy.*[1] Before I read this definition, I simply thought the Pharisee was concerned about the touch of this sinful woman because of the Law. The touch of an unclean person caused the recipient to be unclean for twenty-four hours and unable to enter the Temple. But the definition of *haptō* reveals a more graphic image than a mere touch of the hand.

*Haptō* suggests that her mannerisms are those of a prostitute. This kind of touch manipulated and influenced. I'm not implying anything sexual happened, but I'm suggesting that her movements were provocative to the Pharisee and to others.

Perhaps *he* was aware of her profession. Likely she would have been dressed differently. But even if her dress or his knowledge of her profession were not obvious, perhaps the way she touched the feet of Jesus gave her shame away. There was no other way she could anoint this man. Her mannerisms were aggressive because this was all she knew. This is how she had been taught to show love.

Jesus's response also suggests that this woman had committed great sin in her life. He told the gaping dinner guests, "Her many sins have been forgiven" (7:47).

In contrast, though Mary of Bethany carried a rebellious spirit, there is no indication that she had been guilty of prostitution or great sin. So, despite the tempting similarities which occur in all four accounts, Jesus's words broke my compulsion to link these two women.

Another traditional belief suggests that this sinful woman was Mary Magdalene. She was not. We will tackle this theory in the next chapter.

For now, however, let's go back to Luke's story and watch this nameless woman anoint the Savior. He accepts her gift as if she indeed were the "not-so-sinful" Mary B. Our Jesus is not biased.

Luke tells us (in my paraphrase) that when this woman heard Jesus was in town, she grabbed her best perfume and hoofed it across town to the Pharisee's party despite the lack of an invitation.

Can you picture this woman defiantly and assuredly walking straight in to the Pharisee's home armed with her alabaster jar? I don't think she had to think twice about what she would do when she got to Jesus.

People were always coming to Jesus asking him to heal them or their loved one. But this woman came with no hidden agenda or petition. She simply desired to be near him and to anoint his feet. She came to Jesus to give rather than receive.

Not many people came to Jesus that way.

We know she was uninvited, and we know those attending the party shunned her presence. Yet as she came, she did so without restraint. Read again with me: "When a woman who had lived a sinful life in that town learned that Jesus was eating at the Pharisee's house, she brought an alabaster jar of perfume, and she stood behind him at his feet weeping" (7:37).

The Gospel writer described this woman as standing rather than kneeling, which seemed strange to me. Was she really standing? I wanted to know because I wanted to visualize this scene. In my search to find this answer, I discovered a much richer reason for Luke's choice of words. The Greek word is *histēmi* ('his-tāy-mee) which literally means to stand, but it also means to *position oneself in the presence of a judge or the Sanhedrin.*[2] Our Western brains take each word so literally, but the Eastern language is not as literal. Theirs is a heart language. Perhaps Luke's choice of words wasn't for a mental photograph; it was simply for the heart.

Luke tells us she positioned herself before God himself and the Pharisee—in the presence of judgment—to give her gift. She was *histēmi*. I wonder if her hands were shaking as she knelt down near Jesus's feet. What would it be like to be so close to God? If her hands weren't shaking in the beginning, I'm sure as she began to anoint his feet with the oil, her tears began to fall. She'd never been so close to a man whose body radiated holiness.

In the presence of holiness we become aware of our sin. Perhaps as she anointed Jesus, she began to grieve about the sin in her life. Her body collapsed in a heap of sorrow. Her shoulders shook out of control as each tear fell. She wet his feet not with well water but with her tears. She was *weeping*. This is the very same word John used to describe the scene at Lazarus's tomb.

As we've learned, *klaiō* is a term used for grief and pain. Just as I pictured Mary of Bethany wailing at Lazarus's tomb, can you hear the unnamed woman in Luke wailing as she cried cascades of tears? Tears so numerous his feet were washed by their deluge.

Can you hear both women wailing as they pour out not only jars of perfumed oil but their tears and hearts to Jesus?

We've established that Mary of Bethany is preparing Jesus for burial when she anoints him. If so, wouldn't her tears also have been that of *klaiō*? Can you imagine why these women received unfavorable attention from those around the table? Just as Mary of Bethany's gift disturbed the dinner guests and caused them to become disgruntled, so Luke's heroine disgusted the Pharisee who had invited Jesus.

If we were at this party, would this man's attitude have been as transparent to us as it was to Jesus? I wonder if I would have desired to join the woman anointing Jesus or wished her to leave. Would I have felt uncomfortable watching her worship Jesus this way? Would I have had thoughts like Simon's?

Simon's thoughts not only revealed his judgmental attitude, but they also revealed his lack of faith in who Jesus was. He thought, *If this man were a prophet* . . . . The Pharisee didn't believe Jesus was a prophet, much less the Son of God. However, it isn't Simon's lack of faith that Jesus responded to. Jesus countered his judgmental heart.

Jesus answered his host with a parable.

I love Jesus. He always knows the core of those with whom he is dealing. So he spoke to Simon, using a scene close to this man's heart. It was a parable of two people who owed money to a moneylender. The question Jesus asked Simon was not one that required a rocket scientist to answer. Quite simply, it was easy to see that the one person who had been forgiven the larger debt would be more thankful. Jesus didn't want him to miss his point, so he unraveled the parable and applied it to the lives of these two people both *histēmi* in his presence.

I wonder if Simon grew smaller with each rebuke from the Messiah or if his chest puffed out with indignation. Was he so full of religious pride that he couldn't receive the admonishment with hope for his own forgiveness? Jesus put the religious Pharisee in his place, and he forgave the sinful woman whose movements were provocative yet honest and filled with remorse and thanksgiving.

You see, this woman was blessed because she had come to Jesus. Despite who she was, she recognized Jesus as Messiah. Her actions proved her worship. She came to Jesus simply to love him and worship him. The perfumed oil in her alabaster jar may have represented her old life of sin and shame. Perhaps it had been some form of payment. By emptying all of the contents in this jar, was she giving up her old way of life? It would no longer be a tool in her business, nor her prize possession. She would have nothing. But she would be free.

Her old perfume had been used many times to lure men into her bed, but this night she'd pour out the last drop of her partner in sin, mourn the emptiness of her life, and find forgiveness from a man who was also God himself.

Both she and our dear Mary B. anointed the Lord with hearts filled with gratitude for what he had done in their lives, and both acts of anointing were filled with grief. One woman grieved for her sin while the other grieved because of the coming death of her beloved Jesus. But both came to Jesus with the pure motive of love. It is their love that connects them.

Read Jesus's words with me again:

> Then he turned toward the woman and said to Simon,
> "Do you see this woman? I came into your house. You
> did not give me any water for my feet, but she wet my
> feet with her tears and wiped them with her hair. You
> did not give me a kiss, but this woman, from the time
> I entered, has not stopped kissing my feet. You did not

put oil on my head, but she has poured perfume on my feet. Therefore, I tell you, her many sins have been forgiven—as her great love has shown. But whoever has been forgiven little loves little." (Luke 7:44–47 NIV)

She loved much.

This is not just an ordinary, friendly love. No, Jesus told Simon that this forgiven woman *agapaō* (ag-ap-'ah-ō)[3]. This word means so much more than our word for love suggests to our twenty-first-century Western brains. Whole books and studies have been devoted just to this verb, but I will try to give you at least a glimpse of its meaning.

*Agape* is the type of love God has for us. It is above all other loves because it's not based on common interests, as friendly, *phileō* love may be, nor is it based on reciprocation. *Agape* love is given based on the needs of the person rather than his or her desires or the desires of the benefactor.

God *agapaōs* his children. "For God so *agapaō* the world, that he gave his one and only Son, that whoever believes in him shall not perish but have eternal life" (John 3:16). We can't fathom such love. But when our hearts turn away from our self-righteousness, and we turn toward the living God, we can experience God's *agape* love that can turn ours from selfish loving to *agapaō*.

This unnamed woman and Mary of Bethany anointed Jesus with hearts that loved him with unselfish, open *agape*. When was the last time you loved Jesus like that? No, we can't see his presence, but if you've invited him to be your Savior, he is beside you, and his Spirit is within you.

If you've known him for a long time, there is a chance your love has become more of a day-to-day, monotonous friendly love, just as our marriages can become. If so, kneel before Jesus, confess that self-righteous love, and anoint him and your carpet with your tears as you worship him on your knees.

A very dear friend of mine wrote a beautiful poem about this woman's anointing of Jesus. This friend was one who loved me with *agape* love. She led me back to the Lord after I had spent a year of sin and emptiness in search for the bigger picture. As I close this chapter with her poem, I kneel at Jesus's feet, no different from the sinful woman in Luke or Mary of Bethany, whom I have come to love so. Kneel with me, either in heart or physically on the ground, and worship our Savior who died to set us free. Kneel in the presence of his holiness. May we grieve because of our sin and desire to boldly demonstrate our love for Jesus. We will never be the same.

### Broken Jar

*From a whirlwind of restlessness, in a pit of despair,*
*She searched for a beacon somewhere out there.*
*And waiting to revive her heart from its tomb*
*Loomed diamonds, leather, silk and perfume.*
*She pulled them close to her heart to enfold.*
*These, oh yes, these will bring rest to my soul.*

*But, alas, her entanglement in the trappings of this world*
*Failed to spark and kindle warmth in this frozen-hearted girl.*
*A spirit that is kindred, a sympathetic ear*
*Are all I need to sweeten the bitter journey I'm on down here.*
*So her heart lunged and gathered friends into her fold,*
*Faithful friends will surely bring rest unto my soul.*

*But even bosom buddies can't be near us every hour.*
*And she floundered, close to drowning,*
*crying to an unseen power.*
*Her flesh cried for flesh; It's a husband that I need!*
*We shall cleave to one another as the Bible has decreed.*

*A shoulder I can lean on, someone I can hold.*
*Oh yes, a precious husband will bring rest unto my soul.*

*But spirits intertwined loosen time and time again*
*And threaten to unravel every now and then.*
*Someone to possess and carry on my family seed*
*Is what my soul is craving and is sure to meet my needs.*
*Children are Earth's blessing, or so we've been told.*
*Ah, these flaxen-haired angels will deliver rest to my soul!*

*But flesh is ever flesh, even in its rarest art.*
*And even children try the soul or leave and break the heart.*
*So onto her knees she fell, and with her alabaster jar*
*Strained her vision and found the Light and*
*started journeying from afar.*
*She lavished upon the head of her Lord the last*
*of her heart's perfume,*
*And the shackles fell, and her weary soul arose*
*from its shadowy tomb.*

*Now, she fixes her gaze upon his lovely heart of pure gold*
*And she walks straight ahead holding his hand, and sweet rest*
*abides in her soul.*[4]

## Journal Opportunity

If you honestly admit that you would've been offended or repulsed
by the sinful woman's display of love and worship, write a prayer
of confession to the Lord and ask for grace and courage to love
him as she did.

## Discussion Questions

1.  If you had been sitting at this dinner party with Jesus, what would have been your response to this woman anointing Jesus? Would you have wanted to join her or been repulsed by her?

2.  How were Mary of Bethany's and this unnamed woman's anointings of Jesus similar? How were they different?

3.  What does the word *histēmi* mean?

4.  Have you ever felt as if you were "standing" in the presence of judgment before? When?

5.  The record of both of these women anointing Jesus preserves a beautiful picture of worship of Jesus by women just like you and me. Though Jesus is not present in the flesh with us today, how can we show such love to him?

## Notes

[1] F. B. Meyer, *The Bethany Parallel Commentary on the New Testament* (Minneapolis: Bethany House, 1983), 604.

[2] Lexicon :: Strong's G2476 - *histēmi*, Blue Letter Bible: NIV, accessed February 3, 2015, http://www.blueletterbible.org/lang/lexicon/lexicon .cfm?Strongs=G2476&t=NIV.

[3] Warren Baker, ed. *The Hebrew-Greek Key Word Study Bible, English Standard Version* (Chattanooga: AMG, 2013), 1996.

[4] Jan Doke, *Broken Jar: 365 Days on the Potter's Wheel* (Breinigsville, PA: Xulonpress, 2009), 8.

# Chapter Five

# Mary Magdalene
## Alone with Her Demons

OF THE THREE MARYS, MARY MAGDALENE IS THE MOST MISUNDERSTOOD. HER NAME HAS been tainted by Gnostic gospels and movies such as *The Da Vinci Code*. These villains have made her the wife of Jesus and the mother of his children.

Jesus never married. Christians quickly recognize such heresy and dismiss it as another one of Satan's attempts to bring confusion and doubt as to the deity and purpose of the One we call the Christ.

On a less threatening scale, however, even within Christian circles, Mary Magdalene's character has been challenged. With no proof of her association, she has been named by some as Luke's anointing prostitute. Doubt and confusion are culprits that malign this biblical character's reputation.

Even a few nights ago while my family drove two hours from the airport to our home, as we discussed Mary Magdalene, my daughter asked, "Wasn't she a prostitute?"

I was surprised that my eighteen-year-old was affected by this confusion, but her comment verified what I've suspected all along. Mary Magdalene has been misunderstood for generations.

Maybe her reputation was maligned because of the city she she was named for. The Jewish Talmud describes Magdala, the city where Mary M. grew up, as a city known for its prostitutes and harlotry. The Talmud explains that it was destroyed because of its depravity.

Perhaps the final nail on her reputation's coffin was the founding of "Magdalene Houses" by the Roman Catholic Church in the early 1300s. These homes were established for the rescue of "fallen" women, prostitutes.

Come meet Mary M. based only on Scripture, allowing no Hollywood schemes or misunderstood associations to confuse her character.

Luke introduces us to Mary Magdalene right after he tells the story of the sinful woman who anointed Jesus. Perhaps the close proximity of these stories caused the merging of these two women, but let's read what Luke says as he introduces this Mary for the first time:

> After this, Jesus traveled about from one town and village to another, proclaiming the good news of the kingdom of God. The Twelve were with him, and also some women who had been cured of evil spirits and diseases: Mary (called Magdalene) from whom seven demons had come out; Joanna the wife of Chuza, the manager of Herod's household; Susanna; and many others. These women were helping to support them out of their own means. (Luke 8:1–3)

What have we learned in these few sentences? Is there any reference to prostitution? Marriage? A special relationship with Jesus? No.

This Scripture reveals that Mary *called* Magdalene was a woman with the financial resources to provide for Jesus and the Twelve. After her healing, the wealthy Magdalene, along with several other emancipated women, traveled with Jesus and his disciples to care for the entourage.

Before we continue our investigation, I don't want us to miss the magnitude of a group of women traveling with Jesus. Yes, they were there to take care of him and the disciples, but in Jesus's day, upright women did not travel with male disciples and their rabbi. Yet Luke tells us that these women were with Jesus.

One biblical history website describing Jewish women's roles during that time explains, "They could not be disciples of any great rabbi, they certainly could not travel with any rabbi."[1] These verses from Luke, however, prove that a group of women were allowed to travel with this rabbi. Mary Magdalene's response to the risen Christ (which we will contemplate in the next chapter) gives reason to believe the women were allowed to learn from this teacher—a purpose greater than just feeding the hungry men. But I'm getting ahead of myself.

Back to her reputation: if she had wealth, she didn't need to give herself away for money. She wasn't a prostitute, but she did endure another "shame." Before she was healed by Jesus, Mary M. suffered the control of seven demons.

The Scripture above gives us other clues about Mary M. Some of them are found in her name. This Mary was *called* Magdalene.

We assume she was *called* Magdalene because she was from a town named Magdala. This is logical reasoning, but she wasn't named Mary *of* Magdalene like Mary of Nazareth. Luke introduces her as Mary *called* Magdalene.

The meaning of Magdalene is "tower," pronounced *mag-dal-ay-'nay*. It's a lovely name. Perhaps Mary M. was called Magdalene because she was tall (like a tower) and beautiful like the land from where she came.

Can you picture her?

Her hometown, Magdala, was located on the western shore of the Lake of Galilee, about three miles south of today's modern Tiberias.[2] I've been there. It is a beautiful area. My small traveling group made our way out of the hustle and bustle of Jerusalem to the quiet shores of Galilee where we spent several days and nights sightseeing in Tiberias and the surrounding villages.

I was mesmerized by the lush green hills that rise above the lake. Compared to the desert-colored, non-sleeping Jerusalem, Galilee's quiet lake and rolling green hills provide tranquility that restores even the most exhausted tourist.

This was the land where Jesus ministered to the crowds. This was where he fed the five thousand and gave his Sermon on the Mount. These shores of the Sea of Galilee were the very shores where Jesus called his disciples.

Mary called Magdalene walked these same tranquil shores and rolling green hills, and this is probably where she first encountered Jesus. But it's likely that before Jesus entered her life, Magdalene's life was anything but tranquil.

Nobody battling seven demons lives in peace.

I can't imagine a life invaded by such mental torture. We don't know how these demons manifested themselves, but we can look at the lives of others in the Bible who were also demon possessed to get an image of Mary M. before she was restored.

In the very same chapter in which Luke introduces her, he also writes about a man who lived on the other side of the lake. He too, just as Magdalene, was possessed by many demons.

> They sailed to the region of the Gerasenes, which is across the lake from Galilee. When Jesus stepped ashore, he was met by a demon-possessed man from the town. For a long time this man had not worn clothes or lived in a house, but had lived in the tombs. When he saw Jesus, he cried out and fell at his feet, shouting at the top of his voice, "What do you want with me, Jesus, Son of the Most High God? I beg you, don't torture me!" For Jesus had commanded the evil spirit to come out of the man. Many times it had seized him, and though he was chained hand and foot and kept under guard, he had broken his chains and had been driven by the demon into solitary places. (Luke 8:26–29)

What is highlighted in your mind as you read this man's story? Is it the fact he lived in the tombs or that he no longer wears clothes? Do you cringe as you picture this poor man—dirty, naked, living among the dead?

The demons drove this man into solitary places. The King James translation describes him as "driven of the devil into the wilderness." To be even more precise, this demon-possessed man was driven to *eremos* ('er-ay-mos).[3]

When this Greek word is used to describe a place, it is translated as "desert" or "wilderness," but when it's used in reference to a person, it means: *solitary, alone, deprived of aid and protection of others.*[4] The demons drove this man to *eremos*—regions where no other person would go. He was emotionally and physically alone. No one wanted to be near him.

No one but Jesus.

There's no doubt in my mind that Mary M. was abandoned too. I'm sure her demons drove her to places she never would have gone in a healthy state of mind. Just as the man in the tombs was overpowered by his demons, so was she.

The demons had convinced the man that Jesus would hurt him: "When he saw Jesus, he cried out and fell at his feet, shouting at the top of his voice, 'What do you want with me, Jesus, Son of the Most High God? I beg you, don't torture me!'" (Luke 8:28).

Isn't it just like the enemy of our souls to persuade us that Jesus will punish or harm rather than heal? Of course, we know the demons feared Jesus for themselves. But if they could convince their host to stay away from the Savior, the demons would stay protected.

Perhaps Magdalene also found herself silenced by the strength and lies of her demonic enemies, convinced that Jesus would harm her.

No one brought this man to Jesus. He was considered a lost cause. I can only imagine that with seven demons, Mary called Magdalene was considered a lost cause by her friends and family as well.

Have you known anyone like these two haunted and lonely people? Have you known those the church turns away because his or her twenty-first-century demons seem too strong to cast into the sea?

In America, we don't speak of demons much. Compared to biblical times, the spiritual world here seems rather silent. But is it? I wonder if the demons we fight simply blend into our culture.

If a demon is an "evil spirit," as defined by *Webster*, could a twenty-first-century demon be labeled as anything that oppresses or hinders us from the "good Spirit" of God? I think of modern demons, if you will, as both physical and mental illnesses which take away life.

May we loosely define "demons" for the purpose of this book as anything opposite of life-giving, or that which drives people to lonely places? If so, two such demons are depression and mental illness. They are phenomena that cause people to hide away.

I know the seduction of depression.

I've experienced it in my own life. While in the midst of depression, I don't desire to let go of sadness and loneliness—not at first. It's as if the depression becomes a beguiling friend. I've seen this happen time and time again with many to whom I've ministered. A person stuck in the pit of depression often can't bring herself toward help. Many times she needs someone to bring her to the Savior.

For many years I've ministered to a friend who reminds me of Mary Magdalene. Over a decade of struggling together definitely strengthens a bond, though there have been days when I've wanted to throw in the towel of ministry and friendship. But I'm so thankful I haven't.

I have no doubt that this friend would have searched endlessly for Jesus in the tombs, just as we will see Mary M. doing in the next chapter. But, at the same time, the demons she has battled for so long have driven her to *eremos* places.

Some of the demons have been physical. Mitochondrial disease and a stroke have made it terribly hard for my friend to have the strength and energy to go to church to worship with the family of God. We all need fellowship.

These demons have forced her to be alone.

In her defense, I do know illness and lack of energy makes the mental and spiritual battles more difficult to fight. I've not lived in her shoes. But from this side of the ministry table, I have witnessed how other demons in her life such as self-pity and bitterness made her load too heavy for anyone to bear. Because of these demons she lay on her bed of sickness and pain alone.

But thankfully that is not the end of the story, because through much prayer and the continual encouragement of a few friends in her life, she has made the choice to choose life over despair time and time again.

She has determined to practice worship and thanksgiving rather than to focus on her losses. She still has her dark days, but my friend is starting to hear Jesus's voice and see his face. The hold of the demons of bitterness and self-pity is being replaced by his love.

Perhaps you've been a Magdalene, battling your own demons that have left you friendless and hopeless. Not only have these demons run others out of your life, they have convinced you to hide yourself away.

This pain touches all of us somehow. Let us learn from Mary M. and her neighbor from across the lake. Please take these truths to heart:

1. There are no demons Jesus is not willing to cast out. It's the will of our Savior to free us from the darkness of confusion—delivering us from a dark life and leading us to a life of light and peace.
2. It is not God's will to leave us alone in the tombs.
3. He came to set all men and women free from the bondage of sin and demons, death, and destruction.

We know this truth. Jesus was and is victorious, so why do we still suffer such darkness, even those who have received Christ? The answer is found in one of the best books I've read on spiritual warfare: *The Three Battlegrounds*, by Francis Frangipane. Listen to what he says regarding Satan's authority:

The devil and the fallen angels with him have been relegated to live in darkness. This darkness does not simply mean "lightless regions" or areas void of visible light. The eternal darkness to which this Scripture (Jude 6) refers is essentially a moral darkness, which does ultimately degenerate to literal darkness. However, its cause is not simply the absence of light; it is the absence of God, who is light. . . . Unlike those who do not know Jesus, however, we have been delivered out of the domain or "authority" of darkness (Col. 1:13). We are not trapped in darkness if we have been born of light. But if we tolerate darkness through tolerance of sin, we leave ourselves vulnerable for satanic assault. For wherever there is willful disobedience to the Word of God, there is spiritual darkness and the potential for demonic activity. . . . We must grasp the point: The devil can traffic in any area of darkness, even the darkness that still exists in a Christian heart.[5]

Moral darkness doesn't refer only to outward sins. This darkness is found in any rebellion against God, any agreement we've made with the lies of the enemy. Worrying and trying to control our lives or the lives of others is one such place of darkness because it demonstrates lack of trust in the wisdom and faithfulness of God.

Other sins may include envy, self-pity, jealousy, and failure to forgive. The Spirit of Light cannot live in these dark places. And as long as we entertain such sin, we won't know the entire abundant life Jesus promised. Many of us will continue to struggle and ask why we haven't become new creatures as Magdalene did. But the Word of God doesn't lie. If there isn't evidence of these two foundational promises of our faith, abundant life (a life of peace and purpose) and a new creation, it isn't God's fault. It's ours.

We must ask God to reveal those dark places, repent of our sin, and surrender to his truth. We will then find freedom.

If you fight mental illness, before you slam this book and throw it against a wall, please let me add this: depression, anxiety, and mental illnesses are often caused by chemical imbalances or some sort of brain damage like that from a stroke. And just as healing from a physical illness such as cancer doesn't always manifest itself this side of heaven, so our petitions for mental healing often seem to bounce back from heaven's walls. The healing doesn't come. I know. I've experienced this heartache. But I will never stop praying for physical illnesses or mental illnesses to be healed this side of heaven.

Jesus heals. That is our hope.

I've found myself in the trenches of ministry trying desperately to heal the Magdalenes in my life. There were days when their demons were too forceful for me to bear. Days when I could not even answer my phone.

Perhaps Mary M.'s family and friends desperately tried to love and help her, but their love failed. I naively thought that my love could rescue these ladies from the hell they faced every day. But after years of being beaten and bruised emotionally by those forces of darkness, I realized that only the love of Jesus can bring healing. Mine cannot.

I've found myself asking God to reveal how he deals with demons of depression and self-pity in the twenty-first century, and I've asked if there really is any hope for people locked away in their own *eremos* on this planet void of a tangible Savior. But as soon as I get the words out of my mouth, I'm reminded of the faithfulness, power, and sovereignty of Father God. I quickly confess my unbelief and petition for a greater measure of faith.

He is God. God can do anything, and he has a plan. It's up to me to press closer to him, relying more on his leading, and to pray for the healing of those tormented by many demons.

Somehow Mary M. encountered the healing Jesus. We don't know if he found her hiding among her own set of tombs or if she boldly dared to touch the hem of his garment on a crowded street in Magdala. It's certain she no longer wanted to be alone. Along with her healing, she was welcomed into a group of women who had also experienced the Savior's healing power. What a beautiful picture of the church.

I believe Magdalene wanted to change. She recognized her need for a Savior, just as the psalmist does in the following Scripture. Mary M. and the man in the tombs surely recited such a prayer to God, as do many tormented, lonely, and desperate people today. May we take these words to the Lord for ourselves and others who need Jesus to free them.

O LORD, the God who saves me,
    day and night I cry out before you.
May my prayer come before you;
    turn your ear to my cry.
For my soul is full of trouble
    and my life draws near the grave.
I am counted among those who go down to the pit;
    I am like a man without strength.
I am set apart with the dead,
    like the slain who lie in the grave,
whom you remember no more,
    who you cut off from your care.

You have put me in the lowest pit,
    in the darkest depths.

Your wrath lies heavily upon me;
　　you have overwhelmed me with all your waves.

You have taken from me my closest friends
　　and have made me repulsive to them.
I am confined and cannot escape;
　　my eyes are dim with grief.

I call to you O Lord, every day;
　　I spread out my hands to you.
Do you show your wonders to the dead?
　　Do those who are dead rise up and praise you?

Is your love declared in the grave,
　　your faithfulness in Destruction?
Are your wonders known in the place of darkness,
　　or your righteous deeds in the land of oblivion?

But I cry to you for help, O Lord;
　　in the morning my prayer comes before you.
Why, O Lord, do you reject me
　　and hide your face from me?

From my youth I have been afflicted and close to death;
　　I have suffered your terrors and am in despair.
Your wrath has swept over me;
　　Your terrors have destroyed me.
All day long they surround me like a flood;
　　They have completely engulfed me.
You have taken my companions and loved ones from me;
　　the darkness is my closest friend. (Ps. 88)

Would you allow me to pray for us? *"We are undone, Lord. Only by your power and your command can the darkness flee. Save those who cry out to you! We beg you to manifest your Presence and reveal your mighty authority and power in our lives. Restore and revive. You were Magdalene's only hope. You are our only hope. Amen."*

Please remember to hold fast to the truth that Mary M. and many others were healed by the Lord. Psalm 88 may sound defeated and hopeless, but the psalmist does claim God to be the one who saves in the very first sentence he utters. *O LORD, the God who saves me!*

This psalm is one of the few filled with grief and little hope. Why would such a psalm be found in the Bible? And why would I use it in this book intended to bring encouragement?

There are two very powerful precepts in Psalm 88 that are paramount in the battle against our spiritual enemies. Remember, Magdalene and the man consumed by his demons were driven to *eremos*. The first precept I want you to learn is this: if the enemy of our souls can convince us that we are alone and the only one going through such hurt and loneliness, the *eremos* will become the womb of our pain. We will nurture it, grow it, and even cherish it.

Have you been there? Do you know others who have been there or still live in such pits?

Psalm 88 reveals that emptiness and abandonment have been experienced since biblical times. It reminds us that as we go through such mental and physical grief, we are not suffering alone. There is power in such revelation.

It shatters the mirage a thirsty soul envisions in its *eremos*.

The second precept this psalm teaches is the sovereignty of God. He is the God who saves. This is the foundation of our faith. He is also the God who knows us better than we know ourselves. He is the God who knew us in our mother's womb (Ps. 139:13), the God who has good plans for us (Jer. 29:11), and the God who sent his son to die for us (John 3:16).

He is in control.

The demons named Legion screamed at Jesus when he drew near to the man in the tombs, "What do you want with us?" They knew who he was; they recognized his authority and power. They also knew his purpose.

Do you remember what Jesus told his disciples concerning the reason for Lazarus's sickness when he became ill and Mary and Martha sent word for help? Jesus said to them, "This sickness will not end in death. No, it is for God's glory so that God's Son may be glorified through it" (John 11:4). This is the principle we must embrace. We aren't on this planet for our own pleasure. This life isn't about our happiness; we're here for God and his glory. Our lives are testimony of the glory of God.

When we come to a point in our faith where we place all of our hope and trust in Jesus . . . when we want his will in our lives more than our own (no matter what his will looks like), then he can work with power and authority, and his glory is revealed in our lives.

The demons are not in control. But if they can make us believe they are, their power intensifies, and we're driven to a helpless *eremos*.

Prayer is powerful. Healing does come. Whether you minister to those lost in *eremos* or you are there yourself, listen to the words of a woman now six years healed from bipolar disorder. She is one of the most peaceful and glowing ladies I've met, yet that wasn't always the case. When listening to her testimony, I began to see clearly that the basis of her healing was prayer and forgiveness. Here's her story:

> My grandfather prayed for me. Walking through his
> house, pacing across his porch, he would hold me in his
> arms and pray for me. He had several grandchildren

whom I'm sure he prayed over. However, his prayers
for me were well observed and brought to my attention by several family members when I got older. They
watched him as he carried me around the house, praying ceaselessly.

I never knew why or what he prayed. More impor-
tantly, he never saw the answer to those constant
prayers, because my praying grandfather died when
I was three years old. Never would he see his grand-
daughter disappear into bipolar disorder. I hated that
label. But extreme emotions ruled my life and my family
for over twenty years. One day I would be elated and
ready to take on the world, and the next day I would be
unable to get out of bed. At one point I contemplated
suicide on a daily basis.

Eventually the mental illness was controlled by
medication; however, no amount of meds could make
me normal and able to function well. I was not able to
plan or cook a meal, hold down a job, or even keep my
house clean without help. Twenty years of mental illness
took its toll. On the outside it looked like my grandfather's prayers went unanswered. I was a mess!

When I look back, though, I can see God's protection, because the man I married loved and cared for
me and did all the things I could not. He was and is
patient, loving, and kind. The main reason I could not
kill myself was because I knew it would destroy him. I
consider this an answered prayer, perhaps one prayed by
my grandfather.

A wonderful husband and meds could have been
enough. God, however, had more in mind. I wanted to

be healed, and I began praying and searching for God's healing. I know I was healed from mental illness. My mind is clear. I cook, clean, and hold down a job as a kindergarten teacher with no problems. I take no medications of any kind. Because of what I've been through, I am able to help others with mental illness find healing too. I have to believe that my grandfather's prayers kept me alive so that I could be healed.

However, ultimate healing came after a season of forgiveness. A few months before my healing God laid it on my heart that I needed to forgive people who'd hurt me. I spent almost two months praying about whom I needed to forgive and what things I needed to forgive in myself. Nearly every day, situations surrounding grave hurt and pain long forgotten would come to my mind. I began to keep a journal with the list so that I could, in prayer, forgive each person. Often the feeling of forgiveness was slow in coming. But I learned that forgiveness is a choice, not a feeling. Over time, every thought of persons and situations I prayed to forgive carried a feeling of peace. I have no doubt that God set me up for healing and deliverance through my grandfather's prayers, but he also prepared me for his healing through a season of forgiveness. —*Beth*

I pray that we and our loved ones may join Mary M. and Beth as people who have been healed and freed from our demons. Let's join them with others who can empathize with our past and celebrate with our freedom as we follow Jesus.

## *Journal Opportunity* _____

Each of us has either suffered our own depression and "demons" or we've known and perhaps tried to help those who are living in *eremos* places. Cry out to "the God who saves!" Acknowledge his power and salvation as you journal your prayers for freedom. Ask the Lord if you have agreed with any lies from the enemy. God's revelations will bring freedom. His rebukes never bring shame— only clarity and new life. His Presence brings healing.


If your life is touched by this battle, Appendix B, *Wisdom for Intercessory Ministry*, will equip you with biblical truths and weapons in the fight for the lives of those locked in their *eremos*.

## Discussion Questions _____

1. What has been your perception of Mary Magdalene before reading this book? Has your image of her character changed?

2. Can you relate to this Mary and her *eremos*? If so, how?

3. Have you ever felt the pull of depression and the desire to feed it rather than be freed from it? How did you find freedom?

4. Explain the power of recognizing that you aren't alone in your *eremos*?

5. Why is it important to proclaim that God is the one who saves you, as the psalmist did in Psalm 88?

## Notes

[1]"Women in Ancient Israel," Bible History Online: The Court of the Women in the Temple, accessed November 28, 2015, http://www.bible-history .com/court-of-women/women.html.

[2]Allen C. Myers, ed., *Eerdmans Bible Dictionary* (Grand Rapids: William B. Eerdmans Publishing, 1987), 678.

[3]"Lexicon :: Strong's G2048 - *erēmos*," Blue Letter Bible: NIV, accessed February 3, 2015, http://www.blueletterbible.org/lang/lexicon/lexicon.cfm ?Strongs=G2048&t=NIV.

[4]Ibid.

[5]Francis Frangipane, *The Three Battlegrounds* (Cedar Rapids: Arrow Publications, 1989), 12.

# Chapter Six

# Mary Magdalene
## Desperate for Jesus

MARY OF NAZARETH, THE MOTHER OF JESUS, WAS NOT ALONE AT THE CRUCIFIXION. NOT only was John with her, but other women stood beside her. One of those women was Mary called Magdalene.

I can't imagine standing at the foot of the cross and watching Jesus die such a gruesome, tortured-filled death. I can't imagine watching anyone die that way, much less the one whom I believed to be God's Son, the Messiah, and the Savior of the world. Not only had Jesus demonstrated that he was the Son of God, he gave these people love. Friendship. Relationship. He accepted them for who they were, and in his presence, they were changed, forgiven, loved, and made whole.

He had restored Magdalene's mind. He gave her life back to her and filled it with purpose. With such wonderful memories, but coupled with fading hope, she stood next to Mary of Nazareth, her heart breaking just like those huddled close to her.

Mary M. wouldn't leave Jesus's side. She intended to do all she could do for him, even after his death. She wouldn't let him out of her sight because she had a plan.

Matthew records her actions and explains why she stood at the cross. He writes, "Many women were there, watching from a distance. They had followed Jesus from Galilee to care for his needs. Among them were Mary Magdalene, Mary the mother of James and Joseph, and the mother of Zebedee's sons" (27:55–56).

Magdalene was there to take care of his needs.

We discovered in the last chapter that this was her purpose as she traveled with Jesus and his disciples. She was part of a group of women who helped take care of the Savior. Despite the agony of the job that day, Mary M. was up for the task. With tenacity and fortitude, even with a broken heart, she would not take her eyes off Jesus.

Matthew goes on to tell us that when Joseph of Arimathea took Jesus's body and laid it in a tomb, Magdalene remained close by. Picture her as we read Matthew's words: "Joseph took the body, wrapped it in a clean linen cloth, and placed it in his own new tomb that he had cut out of the rock. He rolled a big stone in front of the entrance to the tomb and went away. Mary Magdalene and the other Mary were sitting there opposite the tomb" (27:59–61).

I love her spunk. She held on throughout the entire torturous day, literally until the end.

It was her intent to properly prepare Jesus's body for burial with anointing spices. But her plan was delayed because it was late in the day, near sunset, the beginning of the Sabbath. According to their Jewish law, they were not allowed to do any work during the twenty-four hours of the Sabbath, which lasted from sundown to sundown. This would postpone her intended duty, so she had to wait until the appropriate time. (Luke 24:1)

The Gospel of John records that Joseph of Arimathea and Nicodemus quickly wrapped Jesus's body in spices and strips of linen when they put him in the tomb. It is evident that Mary Magdalene intended to come back with her own anointing spices. Though she didn't have a chance to wash and anoint Jesus's body the day he died, this would not stop her determination to do so when the Sabbath was over. So she paid careful attention to the actions of Joseph. She knew exactly which tomb he had laid Jesus in.

Can't you see her and her friend—another woman named Mary—just sitting opposite the tomb watching Joseph place Jesus into the new grave? I believe she would have slept next to the stone at the entrance of the tomb if that had been allowed.

All four Gospel writers describe the resurrection and details of that Sunday morning, and all four inform us that Mary Magdalene was one of the first persons at the tomb. John's account is the most detailed. He wrote that Mary went to the tomb "while it was still dark" (20:1). I wonder if she slept the night before or if she'd tossed and turned, unable to find rest. Perhaps she sat next to her door, waiting for the first hint of the sun. Certainly nothing and no one could comfort her. Remember, this was mere hours from the horror of Jesus's crucifixion. And Mary was a woman with a mission; she would find no rest until her job was done.

When Mary M. arrived at the tomb, she was met with yet another problem that hindered her ability to finish the job she longed to do. The tomb was empty. There was no Jesus to anoint.

Immediate fear and panic struck her heart as she ran to tell Peter and John the news. The men returned with her and also witnessed the vacant tomb. Magdalene's fearful proclamation became reality when they arrived and observed the same scene she had described. The men carefully inspected the place where Jesus's body had been laid, then turned to go home, confused and dejected.

John explains their actions by writing that the disciples still didn't understand the prophecies. The men left the tomb, but Mary M. remained.

Many theories have been written through the years, suggesting possible reasons why Jesus appeared to Magdalene first, but the answer is really quite simple. It was not that Jesus loved her more than any of the other disciples. Jesus appeared to Mary M. because she was *there*. She was the one searching for him. She was the only one looking. Her desperation to serve her Savior would not allow her to leave the tombs. She would search for him to the ends of the earth and carry him back by herself if she had to. Read John's words:

> Then the disciples went back to their homes, but Mary stood outside the tomb crying. As she wept, she bent over to look into the tomb and saw two angels in white, seated where Jesus' body had been, one at the head and the other at the foot.
>
> They asked her, "Woman, why are you crying?"
>
> "They have taken my Lord away," she said, "and I don't know where they have put him." At this, she turned around and saw Jesus standing there, but she did not realize that it was Jesus.
>
> "Woman," he said, "why are you crying? Who is it you are looking for?"
>
> Thinking he was the gardener, she said, "Sir, if you have carried him away, tell me where you have put him, and I will get him."
>
> Jesus said to her, "Mary."
>
> She turned toward him and cried out in Aramaic, "Rabboni!" (which means Teacher).

Jesus said, "Do not hold on to me, for I have not yet returned to the Father. Go instead to my brothers and tell them, 'I am returning to my Father and your Father, to my God and your God.'"

Mary Magdalene went to the disciples with the news: "I have seen the Lord!" And she told them that he had said these things to her. (20:10–18)

I love this scene, and I love Mary M.'s fervor. She was desperate to find Jesus. It's obvious she wasn't afraid of the tombs. I wonder if this garden filled with tombs was a familiar place to her—a place she didn't want her Jesus to stay in alone. She longed for him to be buried properly, and she longed to perform that task. But I also think even more than her desire to serve Jesus, she yearned to see him just one more time. She desperately needed closure. One last touch. One last good-bye.

Many of us know this need. We who have said good-bye to someone we loved know the desperate need to see that person a final time. We might fear the last moment with them, but usually it brings some kind of relief, some type of knowing, and some sort of understanding once we've seen the spiritless body of our loved one. As painful as it was going to be for Magdalene to see her crucified Rabbi, it was something that would keep her from rest until it was accomplished.

Mary *called* Magdalene was mourning. She wailed as she knelt outside the tomb. I confess that I had my own soft, quiet picture of this scene when I read this Scripture in the past. But the Greek text uses the same words for her tears as did the Scriptures at Lazarus's death and the anointings of Jesus. Remember what we learned about those tears? The tears of *klaiō* are tears of great pain and sorrow. They are tears accompanied with an outward, physical demonstration of an inward grief. Mary M. is not silently weeping here. No one could have missed her, especially not Jesus.

She had flung herself beside the tomb, her body crumpling into a heap of wailing and burning, bitter tears. As she desperately searched again, the angels sitting where Jesus's body had lain questioned her desperation. Magdalene wiped the tears from her swollen eyes to see these heavenly beings who audaciously questioned her search and her demonstrative grief. Where had they come from? The grave had been empty only seconds ago. Rather than discovering a missing body, she had encountered angels who offered questions rather than answers.

I wonder why the presence of angels didn't clue her to the miracle she would soon find. Why didn't she question them? Why didn't she ask, "Where is he?" But despite their presence Mary was intent on finding Jesus's body. His dead body. With no recorded explanation from the angels, we can assume that Magdalene resumed her search.

As she turned from the tomb, she met yet another person in the burial garden. Mary Magdalene cried out to the "gardener" with hope that *he* had the answers. "Tell me where you put him, and I will go get him!"

How I wish I had more of Magdalene in me. I'm so quick to yell uncle and give up when the situation seems hopeless. I confess I would have walked home with Peter and John and missed the glorious scene she was granted. What was it in Mary M. that filled her with such tenacity to find Jesus? Had the years of being tormented by seven demons given her this persistent spirit?

I believe so.

Some of the most fearless, determined, and brilliant women I've met have struggled with mental turmoil. I've often found myself beside them, begging them to give up and go home. But they didn't surrender the situation until they won the battle or became too weary to continue. The truth is, when a woman has been forced to fight for her life—whether in a bad family, bad marriage, or mental illness—this person, more times than not, becomes a survivor.

Do you know any survivors? Perhaps you are one. If so, you will find yourself easily able to identify with our Magdalene.

With every fiber in her being, Mary M. begged the gardener to tell her where he had moved her beloved Rabbi. Many would have dismissed her that day, convinced that she had lost her mind again, but Jesus didn't let this be the case. After her plea for knowledge of his location, Jesus opened her eyes to his presence. He didn't blind her, as he would Saul of Tarsus. No, he gently called her by her given name, "Mary."

He didn't call her Magdalene.

*He called her "Mary."*

Stay with me in this moment for just a little while longer. The Scripture moves quickly, but can we just savor this sweet encounter before we too move on?

When Magdalene spotted the gardener she turned her face from him as she asked the location of her Rabbi's body. Perhaps she didn't want him to see her tear-streaked, frantic face. Maybe laws of the day forbade her to look into a strange man's eyes or perhaps for a moment she recognized the insanity of this situation. If so, neither cultural etiquette nor shame would stop her quest.

But Jesus didn't need to see her face to know who she was.

Mary hadn't recognized Jesus—her downcast eyes couldn't see his face. By the accounts of others who saw Jesus after the resurrection, he no longer looked like the Jesus they knew before the crucifixion, but I'm surprised that Mary didn't recognize his voice.

She didn't realize the "gardener" was Jesus, until he called her by name. At the sound of her name Mary turned around to see the one for whom she had so desperately been searching and grieving.

Her heart and mind would never be the same. Jesus had saved her twice, both times "in the tombs," in the presence of death and insanity. Perhaps he'd restored her once to Mary *called* Magdalene, but this time he restored her simply as "Mary." He didn't call out her full name as my parents did when I was in trouble. "Andrea Lyn Stone! Get. Back. Here. Right. This. Minute!" You know you're in trouble when your entire name starts the sentence.

Jesus wasn't upset with her.

"Mary," he said.

Our names are significant to us. They are the one thing we carry with us from the moment we are born. For some of us, our names spoken from childhood bring comfort and good memories. But for others, the sound of our name brings pain and hurt. When Jesus calls us by name, however, that name is renewed and restored in our hearts. It is given new life, just as we are—though sometimes he gives us new names entirely.

Both Abram and Sarai were given new names—Abraham and Sarah conceived and gave birth to Isaac, the promised son (Gen. 17:1–19). God renamed Jacob as Israel (Gen. 32:28). The first encounter with Jesus resulted in a new name for the Simon who we know as Peter (John 1:42). And Jesus knocked Saul off his horse and renamed him Paul (Acts 9, 13:9).

There were other times in Jesus's ministry when he addressed people specifically, but he didn't use their names. One such instance was the healing of a woman who had been bleeding for twelve years. Like Magdalene, she was desperate for Jesus. She bravely dismissed the laws of God and, despite her unclean state, reached out to touch the Healer. Jesus was God; he *knew* her name, but his response to her was *not* by name. He said to her, "*Daughter,* your faith has healed you. Go in peace and be freed from your suffering" (Mark 5:34, emphasis mine). Jesus's response restored this woman's place in the family of God. His response was significant to her need. No longer would she be sent off into a quarantine area, unable to worship in the Temple. She could now enter clean and whole. His response to her also soothed the heart of the man walking with Jesus whose twelve-year-old daughter would die during this woman's healing. Surely he would realize the value of this desperate woman's life to Jesus, as a daughter of God. (In case you don't know that story, don't worry. Jesus brought the father's daughter back to life. She was healed too.)

Jesus knows how we need to be addressed. For some of us, it would be "daughter," while for others, we would need Jesus to call us by name. Some of us need our given names restored, while many of us need a new name.

I've always jokingly said that I can't wait to get to heaven where God will give me my real name. I own my name given to me at birth and a nickname that stuck twenty years ago. Almost fifty, I'm still undecided which name really "fits." But Scripture gives me something to look forward to. It gives all of us something to anticipate regarding our names. "To him who overcomes, I will give some of the hidden manna. I will also give him [her] a white stone with a new name written on it, known only to him who receives it" (Rev. 2:17b, addition mine).

I don't know how Jesus will address me when I stand in his presence, but I know this: it will be the name my heart longs to hear, just as I believe Magdalene needed to hear him call her "Mary." *Bitter, defiant, rebellious . . . beloved gift of God.* Surely her name denoted the strength that kept her at the tomb that day when none of the other disciples stayed.

I wonder if Jesus called Magdalene by her name the first time he found her, when she was lost in her *eremos*. And so the memory of that day of deliverance, the memory of the voice that changed her world forever, found her again. A second time. When Jesus called out, "Mary," the name given to her at her birth, she was indeed born again. The name that was once spoken in harsh tones, hopelessness, and dejection, had been given new life.

I don't believe Mary M.'s eyes were opened at that moment to see the Jesus she knew before the crucifixion. I believe his appearance had changed. But her heart was opened to his heart. This allowed her to recognize his voice.

Once Mary realized that the "gardener" was really her crucified Rabbi, she cried out, "Rabboni!" The Gospel writer John kindly inserts right here the explanation "which means Teacher." Can we tarry here for a moment too? It's another short sentence in the Bible easily overlooked.

We assume this name for Jesus was common among his disciples, but that's just the point I want to make. Magdalene did not cry out his name, "Jesus!" She called him "teacher." Mary of Bethany was awarded the position to call him by this name too. I hold on to this response from Magdalene as further proof of Jesus's acceptance of women as his followers, his disciples. They were not named among the twelve men, but I believe her response to Jesus proves that Magdalene and the other women who travelled with Jesus and his disciples to take care of their needs gleaned from his teaching too—not simply over a boiling pot of stew as they cooked supper for the motley crew or as they washed their dishes, but sitting at his feet as Mary of Bethany did.

When Magdalene recognized her once dead Rabboni, she clung to him as if never to let go. It's almost comical. Mary Magdalene is an all-or-nothing gal! It was not enough to see Jesus. She had to touch him. I picture her hanging on to his ankles with a death grip that would take ten strong men to release.

Jesus said, "Do not hold on to me" (20:17). Our English translation replaces the same Greek word that Luke uses to describe the anointing woman's touch. The exuberant Mary M.'s hold was *hapto,* which describes a strong, aggressive hold. I believe (if Jesus had let her) she would have hung on to his feet, letting him pull her around wherever he went until the Ascension.

Though her hold was strong, it included an element of worship. Matthew describes Jesus's first appearance with both Magdalene and her friend Mary present. He writes: "Suddenly Jesus met them. 'Greetings,' he said. They came to him, clasped his feet and worshiped him" (28:9). The word translated as worship is *proskynēo* (pros-koo-'neh-o). This is a very demonstrative worship. To *proskynēo,* a person falls with her face to the ground, throwing kisses to the one being worshiped.[1]

Sometimes I've envisioned Mary M. jumping into Jesus's arms when she recognized his voice. But the definition of this word helps me envision this scene more accurately. There was no romantic relationship here. She clung to Jesus's feet, kissing them and anointing them with her tears. No jar of perfumed oil rested in her hands, but if it had, Magdalene—now restored as simply *Mary*—would have performed the same task as Mary of Bethany and the unnamed prostitute. She was worshiping the risen Savior.

And holding on for life.

Jesus said to Mary, "Do not hold on to me, for I have not yet returned to the Father. Go instead to my brothers and tell them, 'I am returning to my Father and your Father, to my God and your God'" (John 20:17).

Why does he tell her to let go? Will her touch affect his new physical state? No. Jesus's response to Mary reveals his relationship with those who had followed him so closely.

It is obvious he had work to do before he returned to his Father, but I think that Jesus's words to Mary were more than a "got to get the job done" rebuke. Think of how close Jesus was with those who followed him. He had become their friend, both to the men and the women. This meeting between Mary M. and Jesus was like two old friends seeing each other after a very long, hopeless separation.

I believe he was glad to see her too, and perhaps (just for a moment) it was tempting for Jesus to linger in the garden "catching up" with Mary. No, her touch didn't affect the physical composition of his body, but perhaps it could have influenced his heart.

I envision this moment like some I have experienced at an airport. You know, those moments when you will miss your plane if you don't get through the security gate, but you hate to say goodbye. Jesus said to her, "Mary, I have things to do! I need you to do important things too. Go tell my brothers that I am alive."

The next step in the Kingdom plan could not be postponed or delayed. The other followers had to know Jesus had risen.

Have you considered the reputation of the one Jesus instructed to tell the others he had risen from the dead? It's just like our God to choose the most unlikely and improbable person to do the job. He sent a woman who had been tormented by seven demons, a woman not noted for her mental stability, to tell the disciples she saw Jesus walking around in the tombs.

John doesn't tell us that the disciples questioned Mary's sanity, but the other Gospels do. Mark tells us, "When Jesus rose early on the first day of the week, he appeared first to Mary Magdalene, out of whom he had driven seven demons. She went and told those who had been with him and who were mourning and weeping [wailing]. When they heard that Jesus was alive and that she had seen him, they did not believe it" (16:9–11, addition mine).

They didn't believe *it*. They didn't believe *her*.

In the past, this probably would have infuriated Mary called Magdalene. This was a demon she fought most of her life. People never believed her; they just dismissed her as "Crazy Mary."

"Oh, Crazy Mary is seeing things again!"

But I don't believe their disbelief had the power it once held to send her back to the tombs. Now, after seeing the resurrected Jesus, hearing him call her by her given name, healed yet a second time, Mary simply told the disciples she had encountered the risen Christ, and then she walked away. She no longer needed to beg and plead for them to believe her as she once did. She knew whom she had seen. She had touched him, clung to his ankles in worship, and cried tears of joy over those nail-scarred feet.

What is God telling you today? What is your heart telling you as you meet Mary Magdalene, perhaps for the first time, as someone just like you and me? If you have no clear answers to those questions, then please let these words sink in deep.

There is no one that Jesus does not want to heal and cannot use for the furthering of the Kingdom of God. There is no one who is worthless, or incurable, or unusable. May it be noted that the gospel of Jesus Christ resurrected was first proclaimed through the lips of a *woman* to men. God never intended to silence half of his creation in proclaiming his gospel.

Perhaps if Peter had hung around long enough at the tombs that day, he would have been given the opportunity to tell the Good News, but he didn't. Mary did. God is an equal opportunity employer. May we employ our mouths today as Mary did, no longer affected by the rejection of others but unswervingly, undeniably convinced of the life of Jesus.

Tenaciously hold on to his ankles. Worship him with all of your strength.

## Journal Opportunity _____

Jesus knows our hearts better than we do. Can you hear his voice? Are you searching for him? Does he seem lost or misplaced? He is not. He is standing beside you, calling your name. Write a prayer to the Lord, asking for his resurrected presence in your life. Sit and listen. What name does he call you?

## Discussion Questions _____

1. Would you have stood next to Mary of Nazareth at the foot of the cross watching the crucifixion, or would you have been too stricken with grief to be there?

2. Why was Magdalene there? What was her purpose at the cross and at the tombs?

3. Do you think she had "lost her mind" a second time as she searched for Jesus the morning she returned to the tomb?

4. Would you had been so bold and desperate to search for Jesus's body, or would you have walked back with Peter and John, dejected and confused?

5. Magdalene's eyes of her heart were opened when Jesus called her by her name. What would be the word that would open your heart to Jesus? Would it be your name or a word such as "daughter" or "beloved"?

## Note

[1]Spiros Zodhiates, ed., *The Hebrew-Original Key Word Study Bible, New International Version* (Chattanooga: AMG, 1996), 1669.

# Chapter Seven

# A Samaritan "Mary"
## Unfair Shame

SHE'S BEEN KNOWN THROUGHOUT CHURCH HISTORY AS THE "SINFUL" SAMARITAN WOMAN. She is nameless, but recall what Miryam means: bitter, rebellious, defiant, beloved gift of God. Could her name have been Mary? Five divorces make us question if she were rebellious or defiant, and she had good reason to be bitter. Whether or not she was called Mary, her life seemed to reflect the name. Listen as John tells her story.

> Now he [Jesus] had to go through Samaria. So he came to a town in Samaria called Sychar, near the plot of ground Jacob had given to his son Joseph. Jacob's well was there, and Jesus, tired as he was from the journey, sat down by the well. It was about noon.
>
> When a Samaritan woman came to draw water, Jesus said to her, "Will you give me a drink?" (His disciples had gone into the town to buy food.)

> The Samaritan woman said to him, "You are a Jew
> and I am a Samaritan woman. How can you ask me for
> a drink?" (For Jews do not associate with Samaritans.)
> Jesus answered her, "If you knew the gift of God and
> who it is that asks you for a drink, you would have asked
> him and he would have given you living water."
> "Sir," the woman said, "you have nothing to draw
> with and the well is deep. Where can you get this living
> water? Are you greater than our father Jacob, who gave
> us the well and drank from it himself, as did also his
> sons and his livestock?"
> Jesus answered, "Everyone who drinks this water
> will be thirsty again, but whoever drinks the water I give
> them will never thirst. Indeed, the water I give them will
> become in them a spring of water welling up to eternal
> life."
> The woman said to him, "Sir, give me this water so
> that I won't get thirsty and have to keep coming here to
> draw water."
> He told her, "Go, call your husband and come back."
> "I have no husband," she replied.
> Jesus said to her, "You are right when you say you
> have no husband. The fact is, you have had five hus-
> bands, and the man you now have is not your husband.
> What you have just said is quite true." (4:4–18 NIV)

No, she's not called Mary. But I'm including this woman in this book because, like Mary Magdalene, it's possible she has been misunderstood and unfairly treated in the sermons I've heard and commentaries I've read. I treated her unfairly myself before digging into this Scripture, but a deeper study into marriage and divorce during biblical times sheds new light on her character and on the heart of our Jesus, who stopped and communicated with the brokenhearted.

She also earned a chapter in *A Mary like Me* because this unqualified, imperfect woman was used by God in an incredible way. Just as Mary M.—the most unlikely person—was chosen to proclaim the resurrection of Jesus, this woman, a shunned recluse in her town, was chosen to bring an entire Samaritan community to the Jewish Messiah. She was the very first Samaritan evangelist.

Those of us who have been Christians for a long time know this Scripture well. If you are new to the faith, congratulations! It's a blessing to be new, because you come to the Bible with fresh eyes and ears. In fact, I think some of us know this Bible story so well that it's difficult for us to see the scene any other way than what we've read or heard. However, there are some facts I would like us to consider. They will help paint this scene in new colors, and we'll find a common bond with this sad woman rather than throwing judgment upon her sin.

We know she'd been divorced five times, so let's learn what the law commands concerning divorce in the first century. The Levitical Law states:

> If a man marries a woman who becomes displeasing
> to him because he finds something indecent about her,
> and he writes her a certificate of divorce, gives it to her
> and sends her from his house, and if after she leaves his
> house she becomes the wife of another man, and her
> second husband dislikes her and writes her a certificate
> of divorce, gives it to her and sends her from his house,
> or if he dies, then her first husband, who divorced her,
> is not allowed to marry her again after she has been

defiled. That would be detestable in the eyes of the LORD. Do not bring sin upon the land the LORD your God is giving you as an inheritance. (Deut. 24:1–4)

We must take into account the culture and the Law when we study this story. Though the Samaritans and Jews had many disagreements concerning religion, they both acknowledged the first five books of the Torah. Deuteronomy, known as *Devarim,* is in the Torah; therefore this marital command would have been followed by the Samaritans as well as the Jews.

I've read through the Law in the Old Testament and found no evidence of a woman's right to divorce. Yet, I have always read this story with modern-day eyes. Today, women have the right to file for divorce, and this is prevalent and common in our society. Though getting remarried and divorced five times would be extreme even today, it isn't entirely unheard of.

Elizabeth Taylor comes to mind. And what do we think of her? We're probably more sensitive to Ms. Taylor than the Samaritan woman (especially if we watched Ms. Taylor's interview with Barbara Walters). We forgive Elizabeth T., but we assume this Samaritan woman is a terrible sinner.

I admit, I've thrown judgment at her rather than the grace Jesus offered; however, the Scripture in Deuteronomy reveals much. It sheds a different light on this biblical heroine. Can you imagine being given a certificate of divorce and kicked out of your home *five* times? Wouldn't *you* be a little bit desperate?

But I don't think it's desperation for a place to live that makes this woman distressed and in need of a Savior. It's something much more painful. Her shame goes beyond divorce or a sinful living arrangement. I believe the Law holds the key to unlocking her mystery.

Let's think about what we know so far: we know she didn't have the legal right to present her husbands a certificate of divorce. The men had that control. So the question we need to answer is: Why did five men divorce her, and the sixth man refuse to marry her?

The Deuteronomy text tells us that a husband could divorce his wife if she was *erwāh* (er-vah); this Hebrew word means: "shame, disgrace, defect."[1] It doesn't mean nagging. If so, more women would have been divorced! No, this word implies shame or a deformity or handicap. The animals and people with sicknesses, deformities, and handicaps were considered unclean, *erwāh*, by the Law, and their handicaps forbade their service to the Lord. The animals could not be sacrificed (Lev. 22:17–21). And husbands could divorce their wives who were *erwāh*.

Does this bother you too? Does the Levitical Law seem unfair to women? Absolutely. At least, to our contemporary hearts. Before we go any further with the story of Samaritan "Mary," I want to address the Old Testament Law and how we handle Scriptures that don't mirror our understanding of a loving God.

When Pharisees questioned him about divorce, Jesus explained why this law was given. He said, "It was because your hearts were hard that Moses wrote you this law" (Mark 10:5). It's interesting that he attributed the penning of the law to Moses. Yes, Moses sat in the presence of God, his face shiny after their chats. Moses sat with God, so we believe what he wrote was inspired even though we know Moses himself wasn't perfect.

We also must remember the period and culture in which these laws were written. Judged in our day, this law concerning divorce is heartless, but compared to the laws of other ancient nations, the laws given to Israel were ethical improvements.[2]

Finally, whenever I struggle with the "Old Testament God," I turn toward Jesus—the image of the invisible God, the fulfillment of the Law (Col. 1:15, Matt. 5:17). No Scripture can be fully understood or interpreted standing by itself. The entire counsel of the Bible from Genesis to Revelation must be considered, and we always must ask, "What would Jesus do?" or, "How did Jesus handle this?" He is always our answer.

Jesus continued explaining to the Pharisees in the Mark passage, "Anyone who divorces his wife and marries another woman commits adultery against her. And if she divorces her husband and marries another man, she commits adultery" (Mark 10:11–12). I'm not sure if Jesus's words were the first to grant women the right to divorce. By this time the Pharisees had added many laws to the original laws of Moses. But if Jesus did add this, not only were his words emancipating, they were haunting for men and women who chose to divorce their spouses. Jesus completed the Law. He transformed it from a legality to a heart matter.

I hope this helps. Let's come back to the heroine of our chapter and the divorce law we read in Deuteronomy—the law that was likely the reason for her situation. I don't think it was the Samaritan woman's personality that caused her loss of five husbands. I contend that something was physically wrong with her—something women of biblical days considered their purpose in life.

Taking into consideration the culture and the Levitical Law, I have concluded that this woman's womb was barren. Perhaps with each new husband she hoped she could conceive. She hoped her past "failures" had been her former husbands' faults. But after five childless marriages, the truth became obvious. She could not have a baby.

Having children was the very essence of being a woman in biblical times. It was paramount in their culture. Children carried on the family name and the family business.

It's still very important to us today, and I know many women are grieving an empty womb even as I write these words. The inability to have a child often throws us into the depths of depression, but in the Samaritan woman's day, more than depression haunted these suffering, empty women. The ominous shadow that covered their faces and hearts was shame. Disgrace.

There were other famous women in the Bible who experienced this loss. One of them became John the Baptist's mother. Elizabeth, the wife of Zechariah, had never been able to have a child. She was well past her child-bearing years when the miracle of life grew in her womb. Overjoyed by such a blessing, Elizabeth proclaimed, "The Lord has done this for me. . . . In these days he has shown his favor and taken away *my disgrace* among the people" (Luke 1:25, emphasis mine). Elizabeth's words expose the tragedy of biblical women's shame.

Rachel, Jacob's favorite wife, also experienced this shame in her story: "Then God remembered Rachel; He listened to her and opened her womb. She became pregnant and gave birth to a son and said, 'God has taken away *my disgrace*'" (Gen. 30:22–23, emphasis mine).

I believe the Samaritan woman's actions also point to her disgrace and childless state. Do you remember from the Scripture we read at the beginning of this chapter what time of the day she chose to come to the well? *It was about the sixth hour.* She was there around noon, in the heat of the day.

Alone.

The village well was a social meeting spot for women. They came early in the morning with their small children to gather water needed for the day. But this woman didn't enjoy the social event. She purposefully came when nobody else would be there.

Thankfully, none of the sermons I've heard about the Samaritan woman taught that she went to the well at noon because she liked to sleep late. Rather than laziness, however, preachers have taught that her shameful living situation was the culprit that demanded her midday choice. None considered the Law and the possibility that the man whom she lived with could have been a former husband unable to remarry this woman he'd divorced. The Law forbade it.

Shame played a major role, but the humiliation she held in her heart no man could understand, neither biblical nor modern men. Rachel and Elizabeth could appreciate her noontime water run. Their hearts would have empathized with her. It was simply too excruciating to be around the mothers and their children.

Along with slanderous gossip dancing in whispers around the well, our Samaritan woman contended with something much worse—the empty hole in her heart. Black, formed by the disgrace of a barren womb as well as the sting of rejection by five husbands— five husbands who didn't love her enough to keep her as a wife, as Abram did Sarai. This emptiness drove her to *eremos* places.

Scripture reveals God's heart toward women who are barren or rejected by their husbands. Time and time again I've been touched by these Scriptures. God has a soft place in his heart for his hurting daughters:

"Sing, barren woman,
you who never bore a child;
burst into song, shout for joy,
you who were never in labor;
because more are the children of the desolate woman
than of her who has a husband,"
says the LORD.

"Enlarge the place of your tent,

stretch your tent curtains wide,
    do not hold back;
lengthen your cords,
    strengthen your stakes.
For you will spread out to the right and to the left;
    your descendants will dispossess nations
    and settle in their desolate cities.

"Do not be afraid; you will not be put to shame.
    Do not fear disgrace; you will not be humiliated.
You will forget the shame of your youth
    and remember no more the reproach of your
widowhood.
For your Maker is your husband—
    the LORD Almighty is his name—
the Holy One of Israel is your Redeemer;
    he is called the God of all the earth.
The LORD will call you back
    as if you were a wife deserted and distressed
in spirit—
a wife who married young,
    only to be rejected," says your God.
"For a brief moment I abandoned you,
    but with deep compassion I will bring you back.
In a surge of anger
    I hid my face from you for a moment,
but with everlasting kindness
    I will have compassion on you,"
    says the LORD your Redeemer. (Isa. 54:1–8)

Though this Scripture is metaphorical of God's relationship with
Israel, it reveals the heart of God toward women who haven't been

able to have children, as well as toward those rejected by their husbands.

What a glorious glimpse of the joys of heaven. The earthly empty womb will one day enjoy her children. The Lord will fill the grieving, lonely arms of those who longed for their own baby with numerous offspring—never to be lost for all eternity.

What a picture!

Can you also hear the pain in our Father's heart for women who haven't been loved by their husbands? He holds a tender spot in his heart for the unloved and the rejected wives. How many women grip such pain in their hearts today? I know there are many. Some of them are my friends.

Before we go any further, if you are one of these women, I pray you can feel the Holy Spirit wrap his arms around you. He hasn't forgotten. He does know the empty places of your soul. According to Proverbs, three things cause the earth to tremble. One of those is "an unloved woman who is married" (30:21–23). And so with the heart of the Father, Jesus chose to redeem an unloved woman at the Samaritan well that day.

Despite her predicament and perhaps less than pleasant character, Jesus chose to ask this woman for a drink of water. Salvation himself came to her in person. Jesus sat down at this well and waited for a thirsty, lonely, broken woman.

I love how intentional Jesus was. He knew what time she would come; he sent the disciples into town, and he waited. When she arrived, Jesus asked her for a drink. His question started the conversation.

I wonder if the fact that a man asked her for a drink was even more revolting and frustrating to this woman than the fact that he was a Jew. Did she hide her fear and anger behind her religious talk? Did she really want to say in response to Jesus, "Everybody

wants something from me! You men are all alike! Go home!"?
She had been used and abused by men; why would this stranger
be different?

But this foreigner was different because rather than demanding
the water, he offered to *give* her something. *Living water.* Water that
would fill her dry, empty heart.

She thought this odd. I can see her looking around to see if he
was talking to someone else, but no one else stood beside Jesus. Can
you visualize his intense gaze into her eyes as he spoke to her? She
questioned his offer, but his knowledge of her life and the authority
with which he spoke turned her questions into acceptance.

Those who came with nothing to give but their sin and shame,
their sickness and burdens, were the ones who received his grace.
His eyes saw past their skin into their hearts and offered *living
water.* Living grace. However, Jesus did more than give this woman
a new heart, he gave her a purpose.

This part is interesting. The Scripture doesn't record Jesus telling the Samaritan woman to go back to town and tell everyone to
come see him. But her encounter with the Messiah changed her
into a woman with something to give.

She didn't linger at the well after she met Salvation. She went
running into her hometown, the town of her shame and heartbreak,
and she shouted to all who would hear, "I met the Messiah!"

She could have kept this secret to herself. These people had
treated her poorly for a long time. But she held no grudge on this
day. This was the day her value was restored, and that is something
you can't be quiet about. In the presence of Jesus, she was given
significance. Her dignity was given back. Shame gone. Joy renewed.

I want to point out a very important fact: this woman's life situation didn't change. Her joy didn't come from a baby in her arms or
a husband who wanted to love her forever. Her life changed because

her heart had been filled with the Holy Spirit. She encountered Jesus who intentionally met her at the well, and he gave her worth.

In America we've confused the gospel, the promise of a changed life, with a life without hardships, illness, debt, or undesirable living situations. I have come to realize the error and danger of this doctrine. I've watched people turn away from God when life for them is still difficult and complicated.

But Jesus desires to change our hearts first. He won't repair our lives until he can mend our hearts. That place of restoration can only be found when we want our hearts to change. When we recognize our sin and our need for Jesus. When we come to him asking for a heart transplant rather than a new house. That's when the *living water* can enter into our souls.

When the Holy Spirit fills us, circumstantial disappointments fade away.

The Samaritan woman was at the end of herself. She had tried five times to fix the problem of her childlessness to no avail. She knew she needed more than a husband; she needed the Messiah. Don't miss the fact that her need afforded her the honor of being the first to proclaim Christ to the town of Sychar.

Jesus didn't sit at the well at just the right time of day to meet the most influential person of the town. He waited for the most unlikable and unlikely person to choose for his mission.

It wasn't her education, beauty, or holiness that drew the townspeople to Jesus, but her changed countenance. This woman's testimony of joy brought Life to an entire community. How I pray ours will also. May this Scripture become our testimony and our ministry:

The Spirit of the Sovereign Lord is on me,
        because the Lord has anointed me

to proclaim good news to the poor.
He has sent me to bind up the brokenhearted,
    to proclaim freedom for the captives
    and release from darkness for the prisoners,
to proclaim the year of the LORD's favor
    and the day of vengeance of our God,
to comfort all who mourn,
    and provide for those who grieve in Zion—
to bestow on them a crown of beauty
    instead of ashes,
the oil of joy
    instead of mourning,
and a garment of praise
    instead of a spirit of despair.
They will be called oaks of righteousness,
    a planting of the LORD
    for the display of his splendor. (Isa. 61:1–3 NIV)

## Journal Opportunity _____

Have you experienced an encounter like this with Jesus? A
life-changing, joy-restoring, faith-imparting conversation? If not,
it could be because you've not given him a chance to ask you a
question. When we stop petitioning, he can start the dialogue. He
will often begin it with a question. Jesus might ask something of
you, but he will never ask without promising something greater in
return. Don't be afraid. You have nothing to lose and everything
to gain when Jesus starts the conversation. Wait for his question.
Then write your thoughts and prayer.

## Discussion Questions

1. How have you always envisioned this woman? Have you considered her a terrible sinner or felt empathy for her?

2. Who started the conversation? Has Jesus ever started a conversation with you?

3. What was the Levitical Law concerning divorce? (Deuteronomy 24:1–4). Could knowing this law change the way we interpret this scene with Jesus? Can you see this woman as a first-century woman rather than a legally empowered modern woman?

4. Do you agree with the author's theory concerning the Samaritan woman's shame and disgrace? Does this theory change the way you envision this scene? Does it change Jesus's tone or purpose?

5. Jesus lived every moment with intentionality. How can we live that way?

## Notes

[1] Spiros Zodhiates, ed., *The Hebrew-Original Key Word Study Bible, New International Version* (Chattanooga: AMG, 1996), 1542.

[2] Gordon D. Fee and Douglas Stuart, *How to Read the Bible for All It's Worth* (Grand Rapids: Zondervan, 2014), 181.

# Chapter Eight

# Mary of Nazareth
## Afraid of the Call

WOULD YOU AGREE THAT THE BEST-KNOWN MARY OF ALL IS THE ONE WHO LIVED IN Nazareth? Mary of Magdalene's story ends when she's talking to angels. Mary of Nazareth is talking to one when we meet her.

> In the sixth month [of Elizabeth's pregnancy], God sent the angel Gabriel to Nazareth, a town in Galilee, to a virgin pledged to be married to a man named Joseph, a descendant of David. The virgin's name was Mary. The angel went to her and said, "Greetings, you who are highly favored! The Lord is with you."
>
> Mary was greatly troubled at his words and wondered what kind of greeting this might be. But the angel said to her, "Do not be afraid, Mary, you have found favor with God. You will be with child and give birth to a son, and you are to give him the name Jesus. He will be great and will be called the Son of the Most High.

The Lord God will give him the throne of his father
David, and he will reign over the house of Jacob forever;
his kingdom will never end."

"How will this be," Mary asked the angel, "since I am
a virgin?"

The angel answered, "The Holy Spirit will come
upon you, and the power of the Most High will over-
shadow you. So the holy one to be born will be called
the Son of God. Even Elizabeth your relative is going to
have a child in her old age, and she who was said to be
barren is in her sixth month. For nothing is impossible
with God."

"I am the Lord's servant," Mary answered. "May it be
to me as you have said." Then the angel left her. (Luke
1:26–38)

What would it be like to stand in the presence of a heavenly being?
Did Gabriel's wings span the width of the room? Did his body
radiate the holiness of God Almighty just as Moses's face shone
with heavenly light? What did Mary of Nazareth do when the angel
entered her humble, dirt-floored, mud-walled dwelling?

I don't know the answers to my own questions, but I do know
this: Mary was afraid.

But the Scripture doesn't tell us Mary was afraid *of the angel*.
Instead, it tells us Mary was troubled *by his words*; she wondered
what kind of greeting this might be.

Throughout Scripture, angels often admonish people not to
fear when they stand before them. We assume they have to do so
because people are always frightened of their appearance. But Mary
isn't scared of Gabriel's presence. She is troubled by his words. This
begs us to go back and ask the question, "What was his salutation?"

Gabriel said, "Greetings, you who are highly favored! The Lord is with you."

Would you be frightened by these words?

If an angel of the Lord told me I was highly favored by God, I confess I might find myself standing taller and feeling quite special; however, I believe it is the "favor" that troubled Mary of Nazareth.

The Greek word for "favor" is *charitoō* (khar-ee-'to-o).[1] This isn't "pour the blessings upon you with a big house and lots of money and fame" favor that our modern minds may imagine. *Charitoō* implies action; it's a verb that always has an object receiving its action.

When you are an object of *charitoō*, your life is changed. It is the embodiment of divine grace—the essence of Christ himself. We, as mere flesh and blood, can never give such grace. Its only source is divine.

The counterpart of *charitoō* is *charisma*. This is the most commonly used word for "grace." It's a noun. We are given *charisma*, undeserved favor, through Christ.

But when we are granted *charitoō*, there is a "power" that transforms us.

Paul speaks of this transforming grace (favor) that provides blessings beyond salvation in Ephesians 1:6. The King James Version reads, "To the praise of the glory of his grace, wherein he hath *made us accepted* [*charitoō*] in the beloved" (my italics).

We are changed when we are granted this kind of favor from God. This *charitoō*. Simply put, all Christians receive God's *charisma*, which includes his unmerited favor, spiritual gifts, and salvation. But those who receive God's *charitoō* are changed.

They are never the same.

The angel proclaimed to Mary of Nazareth that she had been chosen to receive this divine, life-changing, power-impacted favor.

A favor not experienced before Mary's encounter because it's only found in Jesus Christ. Favor only given through the baby who would grow in her womb.

Mary's life would never be the same.

It's no wonder Mary was confused and a bit troubled by this proclamation, but there was more to the angel's greeting that troubled her. Along with Gabriel's promise of *charitoō*, he proclaimed to Mary that the Lord was with her.

This unfathomable *charitoō* came with the Lord himself. Mary could only see an angel of the Lord before her; she could not see God. Did she fear that God would appear, and within the presence of such holiness she would lose her life? She knew from her heritage that no human could stand in the divine presence of God and live. What did it mean for the Lord to be *with* her?

The angel's presence seemed surreal; no other sounds entered Mary's ears as she processed Gabriel's greeting. She couldn't begin to grasp all that this *charitoō* and the presence of God would mean in her life or to the generations to come.

Quite simply, if she recognized this favor as the grace she had learned from her childhood, she would have realized that this greeting from the angel joined her with the ranks of other favored people such as Moses and Abraham and Noah—three of the Jewish patriarchs.

Perhaps this was also going through her mind when the heavenly messenger told her of the life-changing favor she was receiving. If so, these thoughts could have been the catalyst of her fear. Do you remember what God asked of these men?

Moses was chosen by God to lead the Israelites out of slavery into the Promised Land. But the seemingly short-term assignment became one of forty years in the desert traveling with hot, faithless, and grouchy people.

It was an amazing journey that required an incredible relationship between Moses and God. The Bible tells us that Moses had a connection with the Lord that no other human had. Moses talked with God face-to-face as a man talks with his friend (Ex. 33:11). Yet even after forty years in the desert, Moses did not enter the Promised Land.

Joshua led the second generation of Israelites into the Promised Land, but Moses was only afforded a glimpse into the land he had waited so long to see. It's a lesson Mary knew well and possibly pondered as Gabriel's glow lit the room.

God chose Abraham to become the father from whom the lineage of the Savior would rise, but he was commanded to leave his home country and travel to an unknown land. He then waited for years for the promised son to be conceived.

Abraham did finally hold his promised son Isaac but not without living through almost a century of his own faults and failures and times when he relinquished his faith. It wasn't until Abraham's body "was as good as dead" that God's promise was fulfilled in his life (Rom. 4:19b).

And then there was Noah. Well, you know what happened to Noah. He was chosen out of the entire human race to survive the devastation of mankind. Yet his task wasn't easy either. He faithfully built the very first houseboat, and he waited for the earth to flood, even though rain had never fallen. It is estimated that Noah waited approximately one hundred and twenty years to see God's hand perform what the Almighty said he would do.

Why did Noah find such favor with God? The Bible simply tells us, "Noah was a righteous man, blameless among the people of his time, and he walked with God" (Gen. 6:9). Yet even with such wonderful favor, he had to wait and endure criticism and rejection from his countrymen. As I said before, it had never rained upon the earth. Therefore, God called him to do something incomprehensible. Something never done. Never needed.

The lives of these patriarchs were not easy. Their promises from God not quick. Yet all three of them walked with God.

I believe Mary of Nazareth was a God-walker too.

The Lord is especially fond of those who walk with him. Perhaps this is why Mary N. found herself in the presence of a heavenly being proclaiming her life-changing *charitoō* from God. However, despite such a blessing spoken over her by Gabriel, when Mary stood face-to-face with that empowering favor, rather than responding in wild enthusiasm, jumping up and down like the ecstatic contestants do on *The Price is Right*, Luke tells us that Mary was *troubled* by the angel's salutation.

Was she troubled as a blur of Moses, Abraham, and Noah ran through her mind, counting the cost of these favored men? Or was she simply worried as she tried to figure out what it meant for her to receive *charitoō* from the Lord? Mary's favor was unlike that received by her patriarchs. Not only was she favored as these man had been; she was chosen to receive the divine.

This Scripture is so endearing to me. How many times, like Mary, I've been called by the Lord, but I have questioned that call, feared that call, and despite the promise that God's empowering grace would be given to me, trepidation paralyzed my steps. Yet our God doesn't give up on us if we don't receive his calling eagerly and joyfully. He didn't give up on Mary because of her fearful heart. Rather than giving up, he was prepared for her response.

Gabriel's words unravel the mystery of his salutation, perhaps changing Mary's heart from one of fear to one of amazement. He told her she would be impregnated with the Messiah. The hope of all Israel would be born from her womb. "He will be great and will be called the Son of the Most High. The Lord will give him the throne of his father David, and he will reign over the house of Jacob forever; his kingdom will never end" (Luke 1:32–33).

Do we understand the impact of these words on Mary of Nazareth? Do we fully comprehend the impact these words have had upon our lives?

Upon the world?

After Gabriel spoke, he gave something immensely valuable to Mary. Mary N. did question how she could become pregnant while she was a virgin, but she didn't ask for a sign of reassurance. This is what I love about our Father-God. He knows what we need and when we need it.

Without the petition, Mary was given a sign. Gabriel told her that her relative, Elizabeth, was six months pregnant. Gabriel pointed to a tangible miracle which would erase any questions or doubt that might be lingering in Mary's mind.

Even if Mary had no doubt at that moment, I believe God knew Mary of Nazareth would need the gift of this sign throughout the life of her son. I can't think of a time in her life when she would need this sign more than at the foot of the cross.

Our God goes before us. He is faithful to what we need. He provides the *charitoō* to complete the task given and, if needed, the signs to confirm his grace.

Mary was no Ethan Hunt in *Mission Impossible* on top of a cliff receiving the latest assignment. She was a common Jewish girl from a rather obscure town in Galilee chosen to give birth to the Messiah, the Savior of the world.

She was an unwed teenage girl who had been told she would have a baby.

We must remember, though our society has become numb to scenarios such as this, it is not a desired predicament. In Mary N.'s day however, this sin resulted in judgment, isolation, and sometimes death.

I don't know how well she knew her betrothed, Joseph. Marriages were arranged in those days. Despite their relationship, I'm sure she wondered how she'd give him this news. Her news could result in Joseph's punishment as well as her own. He could be whipped and fined; she could be stoned to death. The Mosaic Law held severe punishments for such a predicament. Despite these dangerous threats upon her life, her family, and her soon-to-be husband, Mary didn't deny the words of the angel.

After receiving his assignment, Ethan Hunt (Tom Cruise) takes off the sunglasses and throws them dramatically into the air just as they explode, incinerating all evidence of the intelligence given. Mary N., however, gave her answer to the Most High King with a humble cry, "I am the Lord's servant, may it be to me as you have said" (Luke 1:38). But before the dust from the departing angel's wings settled, she rushed to behold the evidence of the sign. Quickly she packed a few things and traveled what would have been several days' trip to pay a visit to Zechariah and Elizabeth.

I love Mary's humility and her humanity. Mary's humility is vividly painted with her reply to the angel. I imagine her face down before Gabriel, knees in the cold dirt. The King James translation of her acceptance of the assignment God reads like this: "And Mary said, Behold the *handmaid* of the Lord; be it unto me according to thy word" (Luke 1:38, emphasis mine).

The KJV translates Mary's referral to herself as the *handmaid* of the Lord, while the NIV translates this word as "servant." When I spot a variation in translations such as this, I can't get to the Greek text fast enough. The Greek word translated differently here is *doule* (doo'-lay), which means "a female slave."

In my mind, it's one thing to be a "servant" of the Lord and another to be a "slave." There's a much stronger negative connotation to think of oneself as a slave. But Mary didn't speak these words with dread.

I believe she spoke these words often to the Lord.

Remember, Mary's language was Aramaic rather than Greek. And the language of her heart, the language of the original Jewish Scriptures, was Hebrew—before it was translated into Greek in the Septuagint. Whether her response to Gabriel was Aramaic or Greek, the true meaning of her response can be found in the ancient language of the Jewish faith. The Hebrew counterpart for the word *doule* is *ebed* ('eh-bed).

Mary's heart reply was: "I am the *ebed* of the Lord."

In the Old Testament this Hebrew term was spoken in reference to slaves and to one's submission to God, but it was also used in the context of one who worshiped *Yahweh*.[2] I believe she spoke her acceptance of the assignment from God with confident humility and grace because she was a *worshiper* of God. Her worship of God bound her heart to his.

She had accepted what God had planned to do in her life. Disgrace. Hardship.

She had also accepted the opportunity to be the mother of *Yeshua*, the long-awaited Messiah. The Son of God.

What if God told you that he had chosen you for a "position" on the heavenly ministry team that would change your life?

That would test your engagement or marriage?

That would threaten your reputation with your family and community?

Please take a minute with me to step into Mary of Nazareth's sandals deeper than you ever have. What would you say to God if he told you that your reputation would be at risk if you followed his plan for your life?

If you have just become a Christian, you might have already encountered this hardship, but if you've been living comfortably in the Christian community for years, this assignment would be hard to accept.

Before you think I'm suggesting that the Lord would ask you to compromise holiness or righteousness, please know that if you ever think the Lord is leading you down this kind of path, it's not of him. The Lord will never ask you to commit a sin, but he will always require your worship of him first. No men or idols before him.

God's call may be a catalyst to rejection by those you respect—even people or leaders in the church. I know, because I have experienced it. Even though I believe I did exactly what the Lord had told me, the rejection I experienced stung and still stings. But I would choose the sting of the rejection of men rather than the rejection of my Father any day. And the truth is, the longer I walk with him, the less I feel the sting of their rebuff.

Mary of Nazareth desired nothing more than to be the handmaiden, bondslave, *ebed*, living worshiper of the Most High King despite the danger to her engagement and her reputation.

I believe these words of the psalmist were etched into Mary's heart before she met Gabriel: "I would rather be a doorkeeper in the house of my God than dwell in the tents of the wicked" (Ps. 84:10). How many times I've meditated upon this verse. It seems so very simple and straightforward. Lately, God has given me a visual as I've pondered these words.

When God gives a vision, I always experience the emotion with it as if I'm there. The scene in my mind includes the doorkeeper just standing by the door and getting short peeks of the beautiful room where the guests are entering. Though he only gets a glimpse, he is so happy to be there. He is satisfied and filled with joy.

Have you ever thought about that? The doorkeeper doesn't go all the way inside, but he fulfills his job of opening and closing the door for others who are invited to attend the feast. He can smell the aroma of the baking matzo and roasted lamb, but he's only afforded the aroma. The psalmist says, "I will be satisfied to be your slave." His desire is to serve the Lord and to be near his Majesty, even if only at the door.

Mary of Nazareth shared the heart of the psalmist. She feared the angel's greeting but knelt at the door of the Lord Almighty's dwelling. It's a beautiful scene to imagine.

However, before we put her on a lofty pedestal because of her humility and her servant's heart, let's enjoy one of my most favorite parts of this story, which reveals her humanity.

It's her humanity that makes her character so endearing.

Mary N. had been in the company of the angel who came from the presence of God. She had just witnessed a piece of heaven itself. But even though she accepted the assignment, the *charitoō* that would change her life, she didn't sit in her room waiting for it all to happen.

Mary did what any curious, frightened, and excited person would do. She sprinted to check out the proof that all of this hadn't been a dream. Mary N. packed her bags. She traveled to see with her own eyes the power of God.

The RSV translates Luke's words: "In those days Mary arose and went with haste into the hill country, to a city of Judah" (Luke 1:39). I think you'll find the Greek words describing Mary's actions very telling.

*In those days* was translated from *tautais* (this) and *hemera* (a time from sunrise to sunset—day.) *Arose* comes from *anistemi* (to cause to stand or rise up) and the Greek counterpart for *haste* is *spoude* (to speed, urge, hasten.)[3]

So, in a simple translation of these words, Luke wrote, "This day Mary stood up and went urgently, quickly, to a town in Judah."

If Mary had to stand up, I believe she was on her knees before Gabriel one moment and then, *that day*—seconds after his departure—picked herself up, brushed the dirt off her skirt, and hastily prepared for her trip. She didn't waste any time before going to experience firsthand the pregnancy of her relative, the one person who would believe the story she had to tell. She ran as fast as she could to Elizabeth.

We visualize this Mary, wise beyond her years, quiet and stoic. We picture her as the holiest of women, even if we didn't grow up Catholic. We may not sanctify her quite so highly in our doctrine, but if any human got close to such honor in our minds, she would be the one.

Not Peter.

Nor Paul.

Nor any other biblical character.

Why do we do this? I admit I do it too. I've never granted her deity, but I do experience a great respect when writing about the woman who was chosen to give birth to Jesus.

But she was human.

Just like Peter.

And Paul.

Honestly, if Gabriel stood before me and told me that I was chosen to bring the Messiah into the world, despite the dangers, I hope I would not have said no. Who would have? Gabriel proclaimed that this child would be called God's Son, and he would take the throne of David—restoring the power of Israel. The messenger from God ended his prophecy with the clincher, "He will reign over the house of Jacob forever, and of His kingdom there will be no end" (Luke 1:33 KJV).

*Sign me up!*

Who would have declined this place in history?

I have to wonder . . . how would Mary have responded if Gabriel had told her the rest of the story—the hard parts? Would she have said yes if Gabriel had told her that Jesus would die on a cross? Would she have hesitated?

We'll never know.

In his wisdom God never gives us the details to the call. We just know we've been chosen, and it's for his Kingdom.

But he is always faithful to grant our fearful hearts confirmation—partly for our initial decision but also for those harder days down the road. And in his kindness he gives us people along the way to encourage us.

So many times I have believed that I've heard from the Lord, but I've found myself needing assurance. I don't doubt the Lord, but I do doubt my hearing and sometimes my sanity, and I'm always excited to share my God moment with someone who understands me. I'm not any different from Mary of Nazareth in this department. I would have been on Elizabeth's doorstep too.

How about you?

## *Journal Opportunity* _____

Write a prayer to God sharing with him your doubts and fears and deepest desires concerning serving him. If you do not have a specific desire to serve him, write a prayer of worship and thanksgiving to the Lord for this season of your life. Ask him to open your heart to his dreams (big or small) for you. (Chapter Thirteen will encourage you.)

## Discussion Questions _____

1. Imagine yourself all alone in a room in your home. As you sit in that room, an angel of the Lord appears to you and proclaims your favor with God. What are your feelings? Are you frightened or not? Why?

2. What is the Greek word for "highly favored"? What does this word mean?

3. When have you needed God's grace (*charitoō*) to perform a task you believed he asked of you?

4. Have you received an assignment from the Lord that frightened or frightens you? Have you confirmed this assignment by way of Scripture or some other means, or are you simply walking in faith that it is from the Lord?

5. What is your heart's deepest desire / biggest dream in serving the Lord? If you don't know, it's okay. Chapter Thirteen will help.

## Notes

[1] Spiros Zodhiates, ed., *The Hebrew-Original Key Word Study Bible, New American Standard* (Chattanooga: AMG, 1996), 1887.

[2] Ibid, 1538.

[3] Spiros Zodhiates, ed., *The Complete Word Study Dictionary: New Testament* (Chattanooga: AMG, 1992), E-Sword iPad edition, Strong's #G5025, G2250, G450, G4710.

# Chapter Nine

# Mary of Nazareth
## Run for Assurance

I FIND MYSELF OFTEN REFERRING TO DIFFERENT STORIES IN THE BIBLE AS "ONE OF MY favorites," but truly, the "motion picture" of Mary knocking on Elizabeth's door and receiving her relative's Spirit-filled reception evokes a symphony of warmth and color like no other Scripture.

> At that time Mary got ready and hurried to a town in the hill country of Judea, where she entered Zechariah's home and greeted Elizabeth. When Elizabeth heard Mary's greeting, the baby leaped in her womb, and Elizabeth was filled with the Holy Spirit. In a loud voice she exclaimed: "Blessed are you among women, and blessed is the child you will bear! But why am I so favored, that the mother of my Lord should come to me? As soon as the sound of your greeting reached my ears, the baby in my womb leaped for joy. Blessed is she

who has believed that what the Lord has said to her will
be accomplished!"

And Mary said:

> My soul glorifies the Lord
>> and my spirit rejoices in God my Savior,
> for he has been mindful
>> of the humble state of his servant.
> From now on all generations will call me blessed,
>> for the Mighty One has done great things
>> for me—holy is his name.
> His mercy extends to those who fear him,
>> from generation to generation.
> He has performed mighty deeds with his arm;
>> he has scattered those who are proud in
>> their inmost thoughts.
> He has brought down rulers from their thrones
>> but has lifted up the humble.
> He has filled the hungry with good things
>> but has sent the rich away empty.
> He has helped his servant Israel,
>> remembering to be merciful
> to Abraham and his descendants forever,
>> just as he said to our fathers.

Mary stayed with Elizabeth for about three months
and then returned home.

(Luke 1:39–56)

Words from the Holy Spirit bubbled out of Elizabeth's mouth, and
the baby John danced a jig inside her belly at the sound of Mary's
voice. The Holy Spirit filled the aged Elizabeth and teenaged Mary
the moment Elizabeth opened the door. They both spoke words of

prophecy and praise to God. What an amazing reunion! Can you envision it? God had taken two simple women and, in an instant, employed their lips as prophets.

I am again reminded that nothing is impossible with God.

The lives neither of these dear relatives nor of anyone living in this world would ever be the same. Their prophecies would minister to generations to come in a book called the Bible. And one day their two sons would play major roles in the Kingdom of God. One would himself prophesy to the world and the other would lay down his life for it.

Elizabeth cried out, "Why am I so favored, that the mother of my Lord should come to me?" I wish I could have seen Mary's face in response to these words. Do you think she smiled and sighed in relief, or do you think she felt cheated that she didn't even get to tell Elizabeth?

I believe she smiled. I would have! This is what she had come to find. Confirmation. Reality of the promise.

I think she probably had a much more wonderful moment with Elizabeth than she could have imagined. As she traveled to Zechariah's house, Mary most likely played this scene over and over in her mind, planning how she would tell her relatives the story of Gabriel's visit. I would have talked to myself all the way there, trying to construct the conversation perfectly. But she simply had to say, "Shalom," and by the grace of God, Elizabeth knew the secret Mary N. hid in her heart and in her womb.

Isn't our God faithful and tender? He didn't put Mary in an awkward position with this dear relative. There was no uncomfortable silence, because God prepared Elizabeth for this moment. He filled her with his Spirit and gave her the knowledge before Mary told the story.

Our book is about Mary, but can we camp out here for a moment and discuss Elizabeth? Her pregnancy was a miracle too.

Her story often gets lost in the momentum and magnitude of Zechariah's meeting with Gabriel and Mary's encounter with this messenger from God. Silenced until his son's birth, Zechariah was Elizabeth's definite confirmation of the call, but we quickly gloss over her role. The one chosen to give birth to the forerunner of the Messiah. The one chosen to absolve Mary's doubts and to celebrate with her when no other human would have believed her or understood.

The Bible specifically tells us that both Elizabeth and Zechariah were godly people: they were righteous before God, walking blamelessly in all the commandments and statutes of the Lord. But they had no child, because Elizabeth was barren, and both were advanced in years (Luke 1:6–7)

After she became pregnant, she quietly enjoyed this miracle, keeping herself hidden for five months. I wonder if she whispered these words to herself or proclaimed them to Zechariah, "The Lord has done this for me. In these days he has shown his favor and taken away my disgrace among the people" (Luke 1:25). Her words evoke both sorrow and elation in my heart. I can feel her joy and thankfulness, but her years of being empty and shamed stir up an ache for these biblical women who couldn't conceive.

Zechariah didn't divorce her, despite her "handicap." She was one of the loved wives, unlike the Samaritan woman, but nonetheless she wore the stigma of childlessness.

But God had a plan.

And his plan could only work if Elizabeth were barren and past childbearing years. Luke tells us that Elizabeth never stopped worshiping and serving God during all those years of longing to be a mother. She might have stopped praying for a baby, but she never denied her faith. And God gave her a double blessing—a son and Mary on her doorstep.

Elizabeth confirmed Mary's fate, and she praised her younger relative's faith. The final sentence in her proclamation is one that has spoken to me throughout my faith journey. Elizabeth said, "Blessed is she who has believed that what the Lord has said to her will be accomplished!" (Luke 1:45).

The Holy Spirit has tugged at my own heart when I've heard these words read out loud. *Blessed is she who has believed. . . .* These haunting words have applied to my life, but they are applicable for all of us on so many levels.

Oh, why do we doubt the call God has given us? Why do we doubt that we are daughters of the Most High God, given new hearts and new futures? Why do we doubt that our Father God has a plan for us in the building of his Kingdom?

Perhaps the answer to this lack of faith is that we're not focused enough on the Word of God. Elizabeth proclaimed that Mary N. was blessed because she believed the Lord's words.

As I meditated on this verse, a Scripture came to mind. When Jesus faced Satan in the wilderness (*eremos),* one of the temptations he faced was to turn stones into bread after fasting for forty days and nights. Jesus said, "It is written: Man does not live on bread alone, but on every word that comes from the mouth of God" (Matt 4:4). I've been reminded again of the importance and power of the Bible.

We must claim the truth in our lives. But too often we find ourselves believing what our emotions tell us:

"You aren't anybody special."

"You can never change."

"You can't dream that. It's too big!"

"You can't have victory over that sin."

"You can't be patient or full of grace."

But the Word of God tells us the opposite of what our emotions so often scream. God promised he'd give his people a new heart and his Spirit: "I will sprinkle clean water on you, and you will be clean; I will cleanse you from all your impurities and from all your idols. I will give you a new heart and put a new spirit in you; I will remove from you your heart of stone and give you a heart of flesh. And I will put my Spirit in you and move you to follow my decrees and be careful to keep my laws" (Ezek. 36:25–27).

The Word promises that with our new hearts and the Holy Spirit we are new creations in Christ (2 Cor. 5:17) and more than conquerors (Rom. 8:37). The One who lives in us, Jesus, is greater than the one in the world, Satan (1 John 4:4). And we have been given the divine nature (2 Pet. 1:4). We are seated in heavenly places next to Jesus, even though our feet still trudge in earth's dust (Eph. 2:6).

Can somebody say, "Glory!"

We live in the middle of the now and the not yet. While in this skin, we will have our dark days, but they aren't our truth anymore. Christ is.

May we who have the Spirit of God within us believe these words for all they are worth. If we're living defeated, fruitless lives, we have not believed the full measure of the Word of God. If we believe his Word, we will also be blessed.

I am not decreeing a "get famous or rich in the world" blessing. I'm not an advocate of the "name it, claim it" or "get rich" gospel. This is not the blessing that Elizabeth was announcing either. The blessing Elizabeth was proclaiming over her relative holds a much deeper, richer, and eternal blessing than our twenty-first-century minds can comprehend.

Mary of Nazareth herself declares: "From now on all generations will call me blessed" (Luke 1:48). This word "blessed" again must be studied in the Greek text to extract the rich nutrients of its meaning.

Have you ever wondered why the humble Mary would declare such an extravagant proclamation upon herself? It never settled well with my spirit until I found a commentary that gave me new insight into Mary's testimonial.

There are two Greek words translated by our one English word "blessed." When Elizabeth's voice rings, *"Blessed are you among women, and blessed is the child you will bear!"* she is saying, *"Eulogēo* (yoo-log-'eh-o) are you . . . and *eulogēo* is the child you will bear."[1]

Does this word look familiar to you? *Eulogēo* means to speak well of, to eulogize. It is the base word for "eulogy." So here Elizabeth is saying, "Mary, you are spoken well of and so will be the child you will bear!" This is the term we use when we "bless" God. We praise his name and speak well of him.

But Elizabeth doesn't use the same term when she tells Mary that she is "blessed" for believing what the Lord has spoken, nor is this the word Mary uses as she speaks of her "blessed" state to come.

According to the editor of *The Key Word Study Bible*, Spiros Zodhiates, these verses contain "the most misunderstood words of the New Testament." Zodhiates clarifies that Mary is not prophesying that the generations to come will *speak well of her*, but rather: "The Virgin Mary was declaring that because she was indwelt by God; this fact was going to be declared by generations to come."[2]

Hold on to your seats here because this may get a little confusing, but it's so rich and powerful when it all gets put together. I pray for understanding and clarity within our spirits as I write and as you read this.

When Mary of Nazareth's Hebrew or Aramaic speech was translated into the Koine Greek, Mary's words were transcribed: "All generations will count me *makarizō* (mak-ar-'id-zo.)" This term originates out of the word *makariōs*, which on the simplest level of understanding has been defined as "happy, lucky, or fully satisfied."³

Zodhiates argues that this word means "to be characterized by the quality of God and thus to be fully satisfied."⁴ In other words, he contends that this "blessed" state is only experienced with the presence of Jesus.

This word is only used a handful of times in the New Testament. James uses it in reference to those who are suffering: "As you know, we consider blessed [*makariōs*] those who have persevered" (James 5:11, addition mine).

Jesus also uses this word in his famous Sermon on the Mount. He refers to those who are needy, mourning, meek, and persecuted as those who are blessed or *makariōs*. Jesus said, "Blessed [*makariōs*] are the poor in spirit, for theirs is the kingdom of heaven" (Matt. 5:3, addition mine).

Neither James nor Jesus was speaking of an earthly state of happiness or renowned fame when they employed this word. They were speaking of a state beyond such earthly endeavors. Zodhiates contends this state of *makariōs*—this supernatural place of peace and deep joy—can only be known by the indwelling of Christ.

Elizabeth cried out, "*Makariōs is she who has believed that what the Lord has said to her will be accomplished!*" She felt the presence of the Most High God indwelling within young Mary. Mary was in a state of *makariōs*, deep satisfaction and joy because she had the indwelling of the presence of the very God who gave her life.

But this story reaches beyond these biblical women. The life of God within Mary wasn't only for God's favored one and her relative Elizabeth to know. The life of Jesus and this state of joy and satisfaction would be known by generations to come as we all have the opportunity to receive that new Spirit—Christ's Spirit—indwelling in us. Because of this, we who believe are *makariōs*.

With this knowledge, my soul sings along with Mary of Nazareth to the God of the universe who has blessed (spoken into . . . dwelt within) the humble who have recognized their need for a Savior.

God's words create. They shape and form. When he blesses (*eulogēo*) his children, his words interact and work in our lives. Yet he doesn't stop there; when he blesses (*makarizō*) us, his presence within us brings deep joy and peace.

"In the beginning was the Word, . . . and the Word was God" (John 1:1). The Word was immaculately conceived within the womb of a humble, common girl, and the Word is miraculously placed within us the absolute second we believe.

I am at a loss for words.

Mary, however, wasn't at a loss. She didn't stand before Elizabeth dumbfounded by her relative's prophetic knowledge. Mary of Nazareth opened her mouth and released a melody of praise overflowing from the depths of her own Jewish heritage. Every sentence in her song was a repetition of Scripture written upon her heart as a child.

As a Western Christian, I am reminded of how little we truly study and memorize the Word of God. In Jewish culture, children began to memorize Bible at an early age. They didn't just memorize a verse here and there. They memorized entire books.

Mary N. knew her Scripture well, and it became the refrain of her most magnificent praise to God.

May we learn again from this dear woman? Let us learn to praise God by his Word. This may be a precept concerning praise that many of you already know, but it is worthy of repetition.

We must praise God for who he is, not because of our situation, good or bad. I often feel my words are so incapable of praising God to give him the honor due his name. And the truth is, my words don't come close, but his words will never fail. So I need to know the Scriptures that glorify my God.

Mary N. praised the Lord for his favor upon her, but her praise extended beyond what he had done in her life. It's easy to praise God when he blesses our lives. But she praised God for his eternal qualities. She didn't praise God for just that moment, but for who he is for all eternity and for all people.

She proclaimed his name to be holy—the same words David proclaimed in Psalm 111:9: "He provided redemption for his people; he ordained his covenant forever—holy and awesome is his name."

Her words resembled the praises of Moses, Jeremiah, and Isaiah, who gave praise to the one true God, who shows his mercy from generation to generation to those who are humble and poor, and who fear him.

As I study Mary's words, I am reminded of the words her son, Jesus, would later speak in his Sermon on the Mount: "Blessed are the poor . . . the meek . . . those who hunger . . . for theirs is the kingdom of heaven" (Matt. 5:3–10). Mary's words of praise were from her past, but these very same words would be proclaimed by her son before the crowds of Israel. He would denounce the rich, self-righteous, and proud; he would exalt the poor and the humble.

Her son would fulfill the praise she spoke: "He has filled the hungry with good things but has sent the rich away empty" (Luke 1:53). A rich young ruler would one day come to Jesus asking if he had done all the right things to get into the Kingdom of God. Jesus would say, "One thing you lack. Go, sell everything you have and give to the poor, and you will have treasure in heaven. Then come, follow me" (Mark 10:21). Mark tells us that when he heard this answer from Jesus, "the man's face fell. He went away sad, because he had great wealth" (v. 22). This rich man went away empty, without the Christ. On that day, Mary's prophecy became reality.

As we open our mouths in praise to our God, may we use the praise of the past from his Word and look forward to the day when the truth of these words becomes tangible before our eyes. For example, I praise him here with the help of the psalmist:

Praise the LORD.

I will extol the LORD with all my heart
  in the council of the upright and in the assembly.

Great are the works of the LORD;
  they are pondered by all who delight in them.
Glorious and majestic are his deeds,
  and his righteousness endures forever.
He has caused his wonders to be remembered;
  the LORD is gracious and compassionate.
He provides food for those who fear him;
  he remembers his covenant forever.

He has shown his people the power of his works,
  giving them the lands of other nations.
The works of his hands are faithful and just;
  all his precepts are trustworthy.
They are established for ever and ever,
  enacted in faithfulness and uprightness.
He provided redemption for his people;
  he ordained his covenant forever—
  holy and awesome is his name.

The fear of the LORD is the beginning of wisdom;
  all who follow his precepts have good
understanding.
  To him belongs eternal praise. (Ps. 111 NIV)

Take a piece of this Scripture and meditate on it as you give the Lord all of your praise—praise from the lips of the past proclaiming the truths of the future. Today, let us sing as Mary of Nazareth sang with Elizabeth so many years ago. Let's experience the supernatural joy and fulfillment that can only be found with the indwelling of Jesus Christ. Let generations to come speak of us who have the Spirit of Christ within us as *makariōs*!

## Journal Opportunity

Write down your praises to God, praises of his hand in your own life as well as praises for who he is. Find a psalm or Scripture that reveals your heart of praise to the Lord and write it down. And if you struggle with negative thoughts that stop you from fully experiencing new life in Christ, look up these verses, write them in your journal and on 4 x 6 index cards, and paste their powerful truths all over your home: 2 Corinthians 5:17, Romans 8:37, 1 John 4:4, 2 Peter 1:3–4, Ephesians 2:6. I'm excited for you.

## Discussion Questions _____

1. In Chapter Eight, we read about God's favored grace (*chari-toō*) upon Mary. How do you see his favor upon her in this chapter?

2. Think back about your life over the past few weeks, or perhaps months or years. Can you place your finger on moments of God's favor upon you?

3. In your own words, what is the definition for *makariōs*? How can we be *makariōs*?

4. Are you living a victorious, fruitful life? If not, what must you do to experience the abundance of the Christian life?

5. What is your favorite part of this meeting between Mary and Elizabeth? Why?

6. Does Elizabeth's story give you hope? How?

## Notes

[1]Spiros Zodhiates, ed., *The Hebrew-Original Key Word Study Bible, New American Standard* (Chattanooga: AMG, 1996), 1837.

[2]Ibid., 1345.

[3]Ibid., 1853.

[4]Ibid., 1345.

# Chapter Ten

# Mary of Nazareth
## Mothering Mishaps

ALL OF US WHO ARE MOTHERS WILL BE TOUCHED BY JOHN'S FIRST PICTURE OF MARY AS the mother of God's grown-up Son.

On the third day there was a wedding at Cana in Galilee, and the mother of Jesus was there. Jesus also was invited to the wedding with his disciples. When the wine ran out, the mother of Jesus said to him, "They have no wine." And Jesus said to her, "Woman, what does this have to do with me? My hour has not yet come." His mother said to the servants, "Do whatever he tells you."

Now there were six stone water jars there for the Jewish rites of purification, each holding twenty or thirty gallons. Jesus said to the servants, "Fill the jars with water." And they filled them up to the brim. And he said to them, "Now draw some out and take it to the master of the feast." So they took it. When the master of

the feast tasted the water now become wine, and did not
know where it came from (though the servants who had
drawn the water knew), the master of the feast called
the bridegroom and said to him, "Everyone serves the
good wine first, and when the people have drunk freely,
then the poor wine. But you have kept the good wine
until now." (John 2:1–10 ESV)

Motherhood is not easy. The first few months of my daughter's
life, I lay in bed almost every night crying to my husband, "I can't
do this . . . (sob, sob, sob). Some women are born to be mothers
. . . (sniff) . . . They are gifted at it. I'm terrible!"

My husband would assure me, "I know you can do this. You're
a great mom."

Thankfully, my daughter survived and I did too. I even gave
birth to two more children after her—two boys who have taught
me a lot. Actually, all my children have been catalysts for growth
and maturity. But I haven't done this mothering thing perfectly—
nobody does. Even those women who seem to enjoy staying home
*all* day with fussy children have their moments.

Of course, we never think of Jesus as a fussy toddler. Wasn't
he always as peaceful as ancient paintings portray?

And then there is his mother, Mary. Was she the perfect mother
who never made mistakes? Did she ever threaten to spank her
children in public or bribe them with chocolate or in desperation
let the babies chew nasty car keys to keep them pacified while
waiting to pay for her groceries?

I know, Mary didn't have a car, or keys, or a grocery store, but
you get the picture. Even if it's only in the very back of our sub-
conscious, we feel it. We assume she was a perfect mother. Again,

church history and tradition played a role in this belief—this subliminal message. But Scriptures offer a different picture.

My purpose in this book was never to malign these biblical women—saints in our eyes; I only long to help us find some common thread, some camaraderie in our humanity, that encourages us in our daily faith walk and God callings.

Mary wasn't a perfect mother. This gives me hope. Though my kids are almost grown, attempting trial flights that lead them back to the nest still, it strengthens me to know that even the mother of Jesus experienced mother mishaps. Yet those mistakes did not stop Jesus from fulfilling his purpose. This encourages me. My mommy failures won't wipe out my kids' destinies either. And neither will yours.

My daughter (the one I cried over every night the first few months of her life) is engaged. She was eighteen when I started writing this book, and now she is twenty-three—sometimes dreams take years, my friends. But I digress.

As I was saying, Lauren sat cross-legged on my office floor this morning, catching me up on all her latest wedding plans. My heart spilled over as she told me she planned for the wedding party to be shoeless during the ceremony because they would be standing on holy ground.

Sigh. Tears.

Redemption.

All those years of struggle, all those prayers, all my failures.

She loves Jesus. I couldn't ask for more.

I find it incredibly ironic that weddings are so much a part of my daily conversations as I write this chapter about another wedding—the one Jesus and his mother attended. It draws my heart into the story as I imagine Mary N. orchestrating events Jesus labeled premature. We moms want weddings to be perfect.

My imagination can expand the details of the story as I envision God whispering into Mary's ear the notion to employ Jesus's skills to salvage this occasion. But that would be pure speculation. And though there are times I speculate, and I love to use my imagination when reading the Bible, as a student of the Word and a Bible teacher, I must base my teaching on sound truth. We all must. Nothing in this story hints that God nudged Mary to demand the miracle.

I think it was simply a human moment—nothing spiritual about Mary's motives. She wanted to save the host, their relative or neighbor, from embarrassment, so she ordered more wine—from heaven. Apparently, she knew Jesus could do things like this. It makes you wonder what he was like growing up. Did miracles happen around him that only Jesus and his parents knew were performed by his young hands?

Maybe. But the Bible doesn't tell us any details of those years.

Mary didn't specifically order Jesus to make more wine. Yet what she implied was clear. I love how she did it: "Jesus, they need more wine."

And though her orders were not a specific command, he knew exactly what she was saying. Her tone and her eyes probably filled in the blanks if there were any question.

It's a mother's talent. It's something our mothers developed over the years. Could your mom do this too? Do you do this with your older children?

Jesus's response proved he knew exactly what she wanted, but his answer denied her disguised petition, "My time has not yet come" (John 2:4).

Despite his refusal, the Jewish mother Mary (a little more like Martha at the moment, giving orders) stood defiant and rebellious to her thirty-year-old Messiah-son's answer. Mary demanded the miracle. She dismissed his reply and ordered the servants to do whatever he told them to do. Though she spoke directly to the servants, her words were a rebuttal to Jesus.

She was his mom. Though a grown man, Jesus obeyed. Mary won the standoff.

Have you ever done this? Have you forced your kids or someone under your care to do something they felt they shouldn't or couldn't do? I once made Lauren slide down a firepole attached to one of those fort slides at a park. I think she was only three. She stood at the top whining, wanting to come down via the pole, but afraid to. Fear and indecision kept her feet planted on the wooden planks of the fort. My patience melted in the hot North Carolina sun, and I lost all good mommy control; I gave her incentive—not the good kind. Rather than continuing my positive encouragement, I threatened to spank her if she didn't slide down the pole. Like a miniature soldier she snapped to attention. Her chubby hands clinched the pole, her legs wrapped around it, and she safely reached the ground proud and victorious.

And I felt terrible. She had succeeded, but surely I could have used a gentler tactic and not the S threat. I should have been more patient.

I wonder if Mary had such regrets after her son obeyed her demand that day. After the miracle, the party was great; the master of the party gave the bridegroom credit for amazing wine. But Jesus had told Mary it wasn't time to reveal his power. Surely, their lives were not the same from that moment on. Others learned of his abilities that day. I love the fact that servants witnessed his miracle just as the lowly shepherds had attended his birth. Surely just as the shepherds could not keep his birth a secret, neither could the servants hush the source of the good wine. I have no doubt that this story spread quickly.

I would be remiss if I didn't point out my favorite part of the miracle—the massive stone jars that Jesus used for the wine. Their original purpose was to hold water for ritual purification, an important aspect of the Jewish religion.

After these jars were filled with wine, they could not be used this way—at least, not until the wine was gone. Their purpose had changed. The symbolism of water to wine, ritual to celebration—the new era of grace over Law—shouts in my spirit. It was the sign of the times—Jesus's time—a new covenant coming.

I know I've done a lot of "wondering" in this chapter, but I do wonder if Mary cringed when Jesus chose the purification jars for the miracle. I wonder if she wanted to whisper, "Not those, Jesus!" Did Jesus make this choice with a little smirk? *Okay, I'll give you more wine!*

I know. That seems disrespectful. Maybe he didn't smirk. But it's fun to visualize it. Was it an awkward and tense moment? If Mary and Jesus did have such thoughts that day, I bet they laugh about it now.

There was another time in Jesus's life when Mary failed. That word seems harsh, doesn't it? Actually, it wasn't a complete failure. They did find him. Three. Days. Later! And he was twelve years old. But really, how do you lose your kid for three days—especially, the Son of God?

I lost Stephen, my middle child, in a waterpark inside a bigger amusement park when he was eleven. I was frantic! Minutes before I realized he was missing, my husband had called my cell phone to check on us. He ended the conversation warning, "Don't lose Stephen."

It was a nightmare, straight out of a scene from *Taken*. Okay, well, not that dramatic, but I couldn't believe my husband had the audacity to warn me of this (I never lost my children!) and two seconds later everyone cleared the wave pool, the waters completely emptied of people, and Stephen was nowhere to be seen. My heart sank to my toenails, and the youth pastor (whose youth group I was chaperoning) and I desperately began to cover every inch of the waterpark to find him. Twenty minutes later (which seemed like two hours) I found Stephen in line with another kid from our group. He had gotten turned around with the mass exodus from the wave pool and started walking the opposite direction from where our group was camped out. He had lost us.

Such relief. While I scoured the park trying to find him, all I could imagine was Mike's anger and heartbreak.

*Will he divorce me if I never find his son?*

Mary must have held fearful thoughts too when Jesus was nowhere to be found. *What will God do if we don't find Jesus?*

Losing someone is one of the most sickening feelings in the world. I experienced such panic with my mom after Alzheimer's stole her memory. I lost her on a busy Saturday afternoon in Boston. My heart raced again. Fear made it hard to breathe. But we found her.

Thankfully, Mary and Joseph found Jesus too.

The twelve-year-old Jesus said, "Why were you looking for me? Did you not know I must be in my Father's house?" (Luke 2:49 ESV).

I find the next sentence a clue to the very human hearts of his parents. Luke writes, "But they did not understand what he was saying to them" (Luke 2:50).

Is it possible that up to this point everything about Jesus seemed so very normal that they forgot? Had he become so much "their" son that the fact that he was God's slipped their minds? They didn't understand what he was saying about his Father's house. That seems so strange to me, but maybe Joseph and Mary understood, and the crowd of family members who had gone back with them to search for the lost boy were confused by his explanation.

The Bible tells us that his mother "treasured these things in her heart" (2:51). Mary knew. She just needed a reminder.

He was not hers.

Which brings me to the final mothering mishap of Mary.

The Gospel of Mark sets the scene well. This was also at the beginning of his ministry. Jesus had performed mind-blowing, lawbreaking, and humanly impossible healings. His miracles tested the authority of the Pharisees and his actions dismissed their laws. He cast out demons, cleansed lepers, gave a paralyzed man new legs, and worked on the Sabbath, restoring a withered hand and allowing his disciples that day to pick a few wheat kernels for a snack.

The authorities weren't pleased. As Jesus continued to grow in popularity and teach with authority and power, the scribes began to whisper among the throngs that Jesus was possessed.

His family thought so too. Read Mark 3:20–21 and 31–32:

> Then he went home, and the crowd gathered again, so that they could not even eat. And when his family heard it, they went out to seize him, for they were saying, "He is out of his mind." . . . And his mother and his brothers came, and standing outside they sent to him and called him. And a crowd was sitting around him, and they said to him, "Your mother and brothers are outside, seeking you." (ESV)

I've always imagined that as Jesus spoke to the crowd, a demanding knock at the door interrupted his lecture. The audience began to murmur. Jesus continued his discourse until the knock sounded a second time. Perhaps he gave one of the disciples a nod, signaling for him to see who rudely interrupted his teaching. It was obvious they wouldn't go away without acknowledgment.

But his family wasn't knocking. They were *calling* out to him.

"Jesus! . . . Jesus! . . . We know you're in there! . . . Jesus! Come out! We want to see you!"

Actually, Mark writes that they wanted to *seize* him.

"Seize" is a strong word and aptly translates the Greek counterpart in the ancient text. The word is *kratéō* (krä-'te-ō), which literally means "to take a person."

With each cry of his name their voices crescendoed.

They thought he had gone mad. Really. That's what Mark tells us. They came to Jesus fearing the worst. They wanted to rescue him and to stop this craziness.

Was Mary's heart pierced when Jesus refused and even denied his family? In response to the heckling people outside making a ruckus (Mary and his brothers), Jesus said words that would break any mother's heart. The story continues in Mark 3:32–35: "And a crowd was sitting around him, and they said to him, 'Your mother and your brothers are outside, seeking you.' And he answered them, 'Who are my mother and my brothers?' And looking about at those who sat around him, he said, 'Here are my mother and my brothers! For whoever does the will of God, he is my brother and sister and mother'" (ESV).

Doesn't every child go through those years when he doesn't want to be seen with his parents? Don't all of us remember how as teenagers and young adults we considered our parents outdated and removed from understanding our passions? And those of us who have teenagers and grown kids know how much that stings. I really hate when my kids believe they are smarter than I am. Unfortunately, sometimes they are.

Surely as Mary of Nazareth stood outside begging for Jesus to come home, Gabriel's prophecy seemed so far away—so different than what she had envisioned. When she knelt before God's messenger humbly accepting her new job as the mother of Messiah, she never would have thought her son would face such opposition from the righteous Jews.

*Was he crazy?*

Rather than building an army of soldiers, Jesus gathered a group of skinny fisherman, broke the law, and healed people.

She wanted to protect her baby that day, but another day would come when her momma reach would be too short once more. On that awful day she would helplessly watch him die.

## Journal Opportunity

Mary held many dreams and hopes for Jesus that didn't materialize as she expected. There were also moments when she and her son seemed at odds. What encouragement does this give you as a mother or caregiver? How does this encourage you for your own life when circumstances don't turn out as you planned?

## Discussion Questions

1. Do you think Mary was out of line when she ordered Jesus to turn the water into wine? Why or why not?

2. Do you think she regretted that day? Why?

3. Traditional teaching justifies Mary and Joseph losing Jesus in Jerusalem for three days. What are some of those reasons you've heard or assumed?

4. Have you ever lost a child or someone you were responsible for? Describe the moment when you realized he or she was missing. How long did it take to find the child?

5. Do you think Mary and Joseph could have forgotten for a moment that Jesus wasn't a normal kid? If so, what would that imply? What does this tell us about his humanity?

6. Did you realize that Jesus's family at one time thought he was mentally ill? How would you have handled this as his mother?

7.  Describe how recognizing Mary's human momma moments encourages you. Why is it important to acknowledge that she wasn't perfect?


8.  What aspect of this chapter resonates the most in you?

# Chapter Eleven

# Mary of Nazareth
## From Praise to Heartache

HAVE YOU EXPERIENCED THE DELIGHTFUL MOMENT OF THE CALL OF GOD? HAVE YOU LIVED that moment of excitement and joy overflowing as Mary of Nazareth did with Elizabeth? If so, perhaps you have also known the heartbreaking, backbreaking, excruciating days during the journey. Days when you've wondered if you heard God correctly.

No doubt, there were days when Mary N. questioned it, all of it. Days when she felt unqualified to raise the Son of God. Days when she didn't understand Jesus's actions or the way his ministry was unfolding before her eyes. Our last chapter uncovered a few of those moments.

I'm sure that over the years she held on to Gabriel's words for all they were worth, and she often found her thoughts taking her back to the ethereal moment when she knelt before that heavenly being, trembling with fear and questioning his salutation. But I'm sure Mary never felt greater doubt and confusion and pain that what she experienced standing at the foot of the cross.

I can't imagine the fear that gripped her heart as she watched her boy endure crucifixion. She must have been extraordinarily brave or incredibly faithful. Perhaps she held on to hope that God would intervene and empower Jesus to jump down from that instrument of death. Perhaps she envisioned Jesus leading an army of angels to take the Roman government by force, thereby ushering in the Kingdom of heaven. But then, maybe she had lost all hope of such victory, and it was her mother's heart that wouldn't allow her to be absent that day.

I can imagine watching her standing there, almost unable to breathe. If I were she, my mind would have been reliving the history of my life with my son. His birth. Losing him in the Temple. Thinking he'd lost his mind. Perhaps she stood questioning all that Gabriel had said; if so, she might have had the same thoughts we have when situations don't make sense. *Why?*

Maybe her only hope and solace was a Scripture she learned as a small Jewish daughter. "'My thoughts are not your thoughts, neither are your ways my ways,' declares the LORD" (Isa. 55:8).

I can hear her crying out, *Oh, God, I don't understand! Let me take his place! Why is this happening?*

I'm sure her mind was flooded with memories of the past. Perhaps, as she watched Jesus, the Savior of the Jews and all mankind, die, she realized with each memory that nothing of Jesus's life was what she had expected it would be.

His birth should have been her first clue that his life would not be as she dreamed—that cold, painful, lowly birth. She never expected to give birth to any of her children away from family, out in the open, under the sky . . . much less to the Son of God. She laid the Christ-child in a trough filled with hay—the Christ-child!

Mary did her best to keep him clean in that stable. But when Mary laid him in that makeshift cradle, she knew at that moment that she and Joseph had nothing to give Jesus—nothing but their love. And so, as she stood beneath her dying son, she again found herself helpless and unable to give him anything but her presence.

I'm sure, with the memory of his birth, her heart was flooded with the images of angels and shepherds gathering around this family of three and giving praise to God. Would they come this time? Would they come to proclaim her son the King and remove him from this splintered cross?

Maybe, just as hope appeared in her soul, Jesus cried out in pain and her hopes were crushed again.

*Will he ever fulfill the prophecies of Gabriel?*

He was dying.

Hope seemed lost forever.

*Oh, Adonai, my heart hurts so! Like a knife is cutting it!*

As Mary endured the pain of her severed heart, I'm sure she remembered the haunting words of Simeon, the man of God who held the baby Jesus in his arms on the day of his circumcision: "This child is destined to cause the falling and rising of many in Israel, and to be a sign that will be spoken against, so that the thoughts of many hearts will be revealed. And a sword will pierce your own soul too" (Luke 2:34–35).

Mary's heart was pierced.

The Scriptures give no indication of anger in Mary's spirit as she watched her son die, but I confess that if it had been me grieving beneath that blood-stained cross, I would have had a real heart-to-heart, foot-stomping, angry prayer time with God. My guttural petition might have been, "What are you doing? He is *your* Son! How can *you* let this happen? You. Are. The Sovereign. God! You provided for Abraham. Where is the ram?"

If I tried to slip my feet into Mary's worn sandals on that bitter day when Jesus cried out, "*Eloi, Eloi, lama sabachtani*" ("My God, my God, why have you forsaken me?"), I would have been gritting my teeth, screaming within my soul, begging and demanding for God not to forsake my son.

Then again, there's a chance I would have been too numb to move, to think, to pray.

The angel Gabriel had promised, "He will be great and will be called the Son of the Most High. The Lord God will give him the throne of his father David, and he will reign over the house of Jacob forever; his kingdom will never end" (Luke 1:32–33). Can you hear Mary's heart beating and the questions running frantically through her head? She probably found herself questioning again, just as she had questioned Gabriel the night he gave her the assignment.

*How can this be?*

On the day of Jesus's death, there were no angels in sight. No signs were given by heavenly beings of the fulfillment of Gabriel's words. There was only the nauseating, faith-snatching scene of the Son of God nailed to a cross. It was a day like no other, and the mother of Jesus probably thought it would never end.

We get to see this scene through eyes that know the rest of the story, but at that moment Mary didn't have this vision. I applaud her faithfulness to stand by her son until his final breath. But I don't want us to miss the continued faithfulness and tenderness of our God to Mary of Nazareth during the darkest hour of her life.

The apostle John journals for us an especially sweet moment, a final moment between mother and son as Jesus hung on the cross. John writes: "Near the cross of Jesus stood his mother, his mother's sister, Mary the wife of Clopas, and Mary Magdalene. When Jesus saw his mother there, and the disciple whom he loved standing nearby, he said to her, 'Woman, here is your son,' and to the disciple, 'Here is your mother.' From that time on, this disciple took her into his home" (19:25–27 NIV).

John names the people who are standing beside Mary N. as she watched the death of her firstborn son. Have you ever wondered where Joseph was that day? I believe he would have been there too if he could. His absence supports the assumption that he had died. Mary had already lost her husband, and now she was losing her firstborn son.

The fact that Jesus turned her over to John is also an indicator. It was the role of the oldest son after the death of the father to take care of the mother. Because his own brothers were not following him yet, he couldn't fully trust them to do what needed to be done, so he gave Mary's care over to John.

These are devastating losses in today's society but even more so for the women of biblical times. In the book of Ruth, the story of Naomi demonstrates such devastation. With the loss of her husband and sons, Naomi was plunged into depths of poverty. She was forced to eat of the grain left behind in the fields by the harvesters—the grain commanded to be left for widows and aliens.

If her other children refused to care for her, Mary would soon find herself in the company of such widowed women. But rather than leaving her alone and in poverty, Jesus used what was left of his precious energy and breath to call out to Mary and John, declaring them mother and son. This is such a sweet picture of our God's faithfulness and grace. John lets us know that he did just as Jesus told him to do. *From that time on, this disciple took her into his home.*

Mary N. wasn't left alone and abandoned at the cross that day. Jesus made provision for her welfare, but, by doing so, he also placed her with his intimate group of disciples. Don't miss this rich blessing. It was essential for Mary of Nazareth to continue to gather with the disciples.

Leave the cross and come with me to the day of Pentecost. We are told in the book of Acts that Jesus appeared to his apostles after his death. Before he ascended into heaven, he instructed them not to leave Jerusalem. After Jesus ascended, the group of followers returned to Jerusalem, where they met in an upper room. Look at the list of names of those attending the prayer session. Luke records: "Those present were Peter, John, James and Andrew; Philip and Thomas, Bartholomew and Matthew; James son of Alphaeus and Simon the Zealot, and Judas son of James. They all joined together constantly in prayer, along with the women and *Mary the mother of Jesus,* and with his brothers" (Acts 1:14, emphasis mine).

If Mary of Nazareth was with this group of apostles, she most likely was reunited with her resurrected son while he visited his followers during those forty days. Perhaps she longed to hold him and touch him. Maybe she held on to him as Mary Magdalene did.

Can you picture Mary of Nazareth, the mother of Jesus, kneeling at his feet, holding on to his ankles, anointing his feet with her tears and kisses as she worshiped him? She was an *ebed* of God. Though Jesus would always be her son and Mary would always be his mother, now Jesus was her Savior . . . her God.

The thought of Mary of Nazareth bowing before Jesus is almost surreal to me. It's powerful. Mary of Nazareth, the woman chosen by God to give birth to the Messiah, also needed a Savior. Jesus died for her too.

Salvation itself would have been enough, but God planned to give those disciples even more. And Mary was privileged to experience his final gift.

Look closely at the sweet favor of our Lord.

Mary watched Jesus die a hideous death; she witnessed him resurrected; but she would have to say good-bye again as she strained to watch him float into the heavens.

"And when he had said these things, as they were looking on, he was lifted up, and a cloud took him out of their sight" (Acts 1:9 ESV).

I wonder what she felt that day. If she felt empty and sad, it would not be for long, because God would grant her a gift even better than the conception of the Christ-child within her womb. Truly generations would call her *makariōs*, for Mary N. would soon receive the Holy Spirit with the others.

> When the day of Pentecost came, they were all together in one place. Suddenly a sound like the blowing of a violent wind came from heaven and filled the whole house where they were sitting. They saw what seemed to be tongues of fire that separated and came to rest on each of them. All of them were filled with the Holy Spirit and began to speak in other tongues as the Spirit enabled them. (Acts 2:1–4)

Our dear Mary of Nazareth was filled with the Holy Spirit of her son. She would carry his presence within her for the rest of her life. Hallelujah! Our God doesn't miss one desire of our hearts. He is always faithful and gives to us beyond our wildest dreams. Mary would never be separated from her son again. And just as Mary received the gift of the Spirit, the very fulfillment of *makariōs,* so can we who believe. The Holy Spirit is not only for those followers on the day of Pentecost, but the Spirit is also for us today. We are promised that this gift is for all generations.

Remember, it's only with the presence of the Holy Spirit of Jesus that we can receive this kind of blessing from God. This is a blessing like no other; it causes the empty places to be filled and the hunger in our souls to be fully satisfied. *Makariōs.* I believe Mary once again experienced the gift of joy that radiated from her soul on Elizabeth's doorstep, but this time it was eternal.

I can't imagine losing my daughter or my sons; death is ugly no matter how it comes. And I know that some of you reading this book know all too well the pain of losing a child. As I write these words, I long to convey Christ's love to you. The Spirit of Christ yearns to comfort your soul and provide for you as he did for Mary that day. I pray that your camaraderie with Mary of Nazareth may draw you closer to the living God who has made a way to fill the empty places of our souls with himself.

If you find yourself in the valleys of ministry, weary and lonely, questioning the call of God and all that you believed he had told you to do, take heart. You are not alone. May you draw encouragement and strength in this account of Mary N. and God's faithfulness to her throughout her service to him.

I'm reminded by Mary's story that the only thing God asks us to do is to take the steps he places before us; the outcome is up to him. His ways are not our ways, nor are his thoughts our thoughts. The Sovereign God sees beyond our circumstances with Kingdom vision, a vision much keener than ours. Stay as close to Jesus as you can, hang on to the truth of his Word, and do not be persuaded to doubt because of the despair in your heart. "'For I know the plans I have for you,' declares the LORD, 'plans to prosper you [bring peace] and not to harm you, plans to give you hope and a future'" (Jer. 29:11, addition mine).

The Bible doesn't promise us an easy road, but it does promise us hope and the presence of Jesus through his Holy Spirit within us.

Finally, if you have believed that God gave his word for a loved one's healing, but that person didn't live, you and I can also join hearts with Mary of Nazareth as she stood at the cross. I know the questions running frantically in one's head when the events before your eyes don't line up with what you expected.

The Lord had spoken to three of my friends and me of my sister's victory over a second battle with cancer. I believed with all my heart. I've never had so much faith. But with each day, the cancer ate away her life. She aged forty years before my eyes, and at last, I had to tell her good-bye. It was the hardest thing I've had to do.

Mary only had to wait three days to see Jesus rise from the grave. I will have to wait longer to see my sister. But I will cling to the goodness of my God and the hope of resurrected bodies when all is restored and renewed. Mary's narrative is a foreshadowing of what we will experience when Jesus returns. We will see our loved ones again.

We must trust in the goodness and wisdom of the Sovereign God even when we don't understand. We must wait in expectation of the new heaven and new earth. Until then, let us be filled daily with more and more of his Holy Spirit, the promise of what is yet to come. Hallelujah!

## Journal Opportunity

If you are struggling in ministry or the calling of God upon your life, or if you have lost a child or loved one, write down your thoughts and feelings to the Lord. Ask him to fill you with his Spirit. The infilling of the Spirit strengthens, heals, and can fill the empty places of our hearts.

## Discussion Questions

1. Have you doubted the call of God on your life due to unfavorable circumstances or difficulty? What were those difficult moments?

2. Did you come through that difficult season, or are you still in it?

3. If you have come through, what helped you the most during the agony and doubt?

4. Despite Jesus's death, what was evidence of God's continued favor upon Mary?

5. Is God still working his favor and faithfulness today? How is he demonstrating such favor or faithfulness to you in the midst of despair, doubt, and heartbreak?

# Chapter Twelve

# *Jesus*
## Empowering Faithfulness

*"If we are faithless, he will remain faithful,*
*for he cannot disown himself."*

2 Timothy 2:13

SOMETIMES (OKAY, MOST OF THE TIME) WHEN YOU FOLLOW THE VOICE OF GOD—THE CALL— you have to do so one step at a time, unsure of God's point or the final outcome of his plan. Writing this book was no different.

Though I wrote this book to help women realize that God loves us as we are and desires to have us join his ministry team, the second purpose (and I believe the most important) is for us to witness the *faithfulness* of Jesus and his empowering grace. This book boasts Mary's name in the title, but it's all about Jesus. He's the reason I write and speak and teach. He's my source. His faithfulness brought this book to fruition, just as his faithfulness empowered the Marys.

We've already visited some of Jesus's faithful moments with these women, but I can't think of a better way to end this little book of faith than to close with a feast of memories of the faithfulness of Jesus and how it affected these women.

Mary of Nazareth didn't seem to have any flaws in her nature when studied from afar, but we did see just how very human she was when she ran to Elizabeth's home to check out the validity of Gabriel's words. We are even told she stayed with Elizabeth, who was in her sixth month of pregnancy. "Mary stayed with Elizabeth for about three months and then returned home" (Luke 1:56).

Why do you think she stayed with Elizabeth for three months? Well, according to my mathematically brilliant mind, she stayed long enough to actually witness the birth of Gabriel's promised sign. Perhaps she even got to touch and hold that baby, who was for Mary of Nazareth total, complete, tangible confirmation that she too would soon hold a baby of her very own. She would hold her baby named Jesus. The long-awaited Messiah.

After three months she returned home. I wonder if it was an uncomfortable homecoming, or if Zechariah's and Elizabeth's miracle gave Mary leverage as she explained her pregnancy and her visit from Gabriel. Now freed to speak, Zechariah was released to tell of his encounter too. Perhaps this persuaded Mary's family to believe her story. Whether it was a tense moment or not, Mary did go home.

Home.

We all need to go home, don't we?

When I think of home, I think of going back to the area where I grew up and to family. I realize in this transient American culture, life often disrupts what used to be "home" to us. Change is inevitable. Whether we embrace change or not, life happens, and home becomes someplace other than our birthplace. Whether it's divorce, death, or a move that causes change, for some the word "home" may be rather vague. But regardless of what "home" specifically means to you, I think we all can visualize it as a place where we have history and find security.

After Mary spent three months with Elizabeth, she did go home, but we are told that when it was time for the baby to be born, she packed her bags and traveled to Bethlehem with Joseph because of a census that was being taken. Each man traveled back to his family's hometown. This means Mary traveled with Joseph, without her immediate family, near the time of her baby's arrival, to a town not her own. She would give birth to her son with only strangers and Joseph by her side.

And . . . can we just talk about this kind of traveling for a minute? Mary, great with child, rode a donkey over bumps and rocks for eighty miles. Eighty miles! I don't fare well when I'm tired. If I had been Mary—my swollen body contracting and threatening to birth a child, when we reached the bustling Bethlehem I would have thrown a temper tantrum demanding a room. I probably would have yelled at Joseph. I certainly would not have resembled the peaceful Mary in my nativity set.

Has it ever occurred to anyone how nothing about Jesus's life and purpose was easy? Even his birth took place in hardship by our human standards. But then again, maybe God just wanted his creation to witness Hope being born. Each star named by God held its breath as the Son of God arrived. Could creation itself imagine how this story of redemption would run its course? How it would end in death?

No one could. Especially Mary. But God was faithful to her despite some bumps and disappointments along the way, such as not having her family beside her when Jesus was born. Now, in this modern era, this isn't that big a deal. I was a military wife who prayed for my husband to be home from Desert Storm to be by my side when our first child was born. In fact, I was prepared to write the President of the United States and petition for his homecoming.

I *needed* him with me!

Without petition, however, he made it home in time for Lamaze classes. But my point is that not all of us insist or want our mother and family to be there when we give birth. After the baby comes home is another story. That's when I really needed and wanted my momma! My husband was desperate for her help too.

Families lived side-by-side in biblical times. And because of this, I believe Mary ached to have her family experience the remarkable birth of her son. If I had birthed the Christ-child, I would have wanted to share that experience with the people I loved. But none of her family would witness the angels, the shepherds, and the gloriously humble birth. There were no cell phones to call family or capture the moment in pictures or video.

She was surrounded by strangers. Shepherds who had been told of the birth of her special child. That would be her only fame that night. Her only source of assurance.

After the birth of Jesus, the Gospel of Matthew tells us, Joseph was warned in a dream to flee to Egypt with his precious wife and child (Matt. 2:13). He didn't wait until morning. They fled to Egypt under the cover of the dark night. Can you imagine the fear in Mary's heart? She had no time to prepare. She quickly packed her bags again and traveled to a foreign country even farther away from family in order to protect their precious child.

However, God didn't leave her in that distant place. We are told by Matthew that the little family fled to Egypt, then came back to Judea, but they were warned again of danger and returned to Galilee, where they made their permanent home back in Nazareth.

> After Herod died, an angel of the Lord appeared in a dream to Joseph in Egypt and said, "Get up, take the child and his mother and go to the land of Israel, for those who were trying to take the child's life are dead."

So he got up, took the child and his mother and went to the land of Israel. But when he heard that Archelaus was reigning in Judea in place of his father Herod, he was afraid to go there. Having been warned in a dream, he withdrew to the district of Galilee, and he went and lived in a town called Nazareth. So was fulfilled what was said through the prophets: "He will be called a Nazarene." (Matt. 2:19–23)

Nazareth.

After running and fleeing for their lives and the life of their baby, Mary got to go home to stay. We read these words so quickly in Matthew that they are easily overlooked.

But then again, I confess that I often miss the small things, the seemingly insignificant things, that prove the faithfulness of God in my life.

Mary, the humble handmaiden of God, who had graciously agreed to have his Son, to rear a child who would be both God and man . . . *this* Mary was given an assignment from the Lord. But the assignment wasn't given without the strength and means to carry it through, with grace along the way.

It had been prophesied that the Messiah would come from Nazareth, but what a sweet "coincidence of the Lord" to have Mary receive the blessings of not only birthing the Christ-child, but also rearing him beside her family.

This may not appear as great faithfulness to you, but after twenty years away from home, the loss of my mom and sister, and the firsthand knowledge of homesickness, I'm blessed to see God's faithfulness to Mary of Nazareth. She didn't have to bring her son up in Egypt or even in Jerusalem. Instead she was allowed to rear her family in the hills of Galilee where she had run up and down the grassy hills in her own childhood.

There's no place like home.

In my own life, when I feel the itch of homesickness, something happens to expedite my trip there. I seem to find myself telling God one day that I want to go home and a few weeks later I learn of something that calls for immediate plane tickets. Tickets that wouldn't have been purchased just for a homesick heart but seem appropriate for a definite family crisis. This sounds rather morbid, but it isn't. To me, it is the faithfulness of Jesus.

Perhaps he puts the itch of homesickness in my heart ahead of time to prepare me for the decision to buy those tickets rather than leaving me to hem and haw as I try to decide if I should go. Either way, I believe it is another trace of the sweet faithfulness of my God who always allows me to return home when I need it most.

One October I felt an extreme urgency to go home because my sister's mother-in-law was dying of stomach cancer. I thought God was sending me to share the gospel with her just in case she wasn't ready for heaven. When I got there, one of her friends had already shared the gospel and prayed with her before I arrived. So I wondered why I'd felt such urgency. I had no idea my visit with my sister would be the last week she felt well. It would be the last few days before she fell very ill.

Christy went to the doctor for pneumonia not long after I left—a pneumonia she couldn't beat. She was diagnosed with stage four lung cancer one month after my visit, and though we had hope she would survive, she would never be the same spunky sister I loved. I would go back to stay with her three more times before she died, but none of those visits were normal. God allowed us to have a wonderful long weekend of shopping and laughing together before tragedy hit. I thought I was there to see her mother-in-law, but God was faithfully giving my sister and me time before she got sick.

I needed to go home.

Even though Matthew 8:20 tells us Jesus had no place to lay his head, I do believe there was one place that was home away from home to him as he traveled around the countryside proclaiming the Kingdom of God. It was in a town where he often stopped and found refreshment and rest for the night.

He seemed to be very close to one family in the town of Bethany. You know this family. We've already attended two dinner parties with them and witnessed the resurrection of their dead brother, Lazarus. We've also observed Jesus's faithfulness to Mary of Bethany when she dared to sit at his feet as a disciple, and as she worshiped him with perfumed oil and tears.

I want us to remember, however, that he was always faithful to her and her family, even when it appeared that he was not answering their petitions to heal Lazarus. If Jesus had come back earlier, neither the sisters nor the rest of Bethany would have witnessed one of the greatest miracles performed in their town. The glory of God, the power of Jesus, would not have been revealed, and we wouldn't have experienced through this record the tears of our Savior, who cried with Mary B. as she grieved over the death of her brother.

Jesus was and is so faithful. Despite Mary's own bitterness caused by her limited perception of Jesus's lack of action, Jesus was faithful. He healed Lazarus and brought him back to life despite the lack of faith of those who didn't understand.

Friends, if he will do that for Mary of Bethany, he will do so for us. He is faithful even when we are faithless. He will show up and be God despite our faith or lack thereof, because that is who he is. Jesus's work in our lives is not dependent upon the greatness of our faith; it is only dependent on who *he* is.

In story after story, from the Old Testament to the New, we witness God's faithfulness. If we keep on remembering who Jesus is, his faithfulness will continue to be revealed. He is the Son of God, yet also God himself, incarnate on this tiny planet called earth.

He is *Yeshua,* the Messiah, who came to save all mankind by dying on a cross. He is the Savior who didn't remain dead in the tomb, but who rose from the dead as prophesied.

He revealed himself to his disciples, first of all to Mary Magdalene. What kind of Savior would reveal himself as resurrected to a woman who had been mentally ill?

Yet again, Jesus's actions were not dependent upon Mary Magdalene's reputation of competence with the disciples or her faith. She was trying to find and prepare his *dead* body for burial. No, Jesus's actions were faithful to her needs, her tenacious search for him, and quite simply to who he was, the risen Messiah.

He didn't hide himself because of the lack of faith of those who once believed he was God. He had to show himself risen because that was who he was and is!

The faithfulness of Jesus is not based upon our faith. Hallelujah! Thank you, Lord. The faithfulness of Jesus is not based on our own strengths.

These stories prove that the faithfulness of Jesus is based upon our weaknesses.

Isn't it true that when we fail, then we know that the good is from the Lord? When we are weak, we then can be strong only through the loving power of Jesus. This is who he chooses to work through—the weak. When we are weak, he is strong in us (2 Cor. 12:9–10). What looks like failure in the world's eyes is an opportunity for the power of Jesus.

When our blemishes, blunders, and personality flaws find themselves in the radiance of Jesus, they no longer look ugly. Mary of Nazareth's endearing run to Elizabeth made her a tangible, real girl to those of us who needed to know that God uses those who question the call upon our lives. He didn't cut her off from his presence. Nor from the gift of God in her womb. He gave her this valuable sign, knowing she would need some evidence of Gabriel's proclamation.

Again, Jesus didn't condemn either Mary of Bethany or Mary Magdalene for their lack of faith. When these women found themselves exhausted with grief, unable to sleep, with unanswerable questions running endless circles in their minds—when these women were experiencing the darkest hours of their lives, the power of resurrection ran through Jesus's veins despite their lack of faith and understanding.

I know I have said it before, but please let me say it again. Jesus didn't reprimand them, but he met them right smack in the middle of their lack of faith and displayed to them the glorious, incomprehensible power of God. I believe both of these women walked away from these incredibly intimate moments with Jesus with the same personalities they had before, but with personalities now empowered by his grace. They experienced his *charitoō*.

I am always amazed when God employs this girl from the plains of Southwest Oklahoma, who fights her own fears and insecurities, to bring the message of Christ to other women and men. I often find myself giving God reasons why I can't speak or write for him. I argue with him about whether or not I should add certain things to my conferences. I tell the Lord I'm not talented enough.

To this God always replies, "You're right. You have nothing to give but me. And I am faithful." Those words are the most freeing words I can ever hear. It's not about me. It wasn't about these biblical women either. It's all about Jesus.

I pray you have received a bountiful gift of fresh understanding and truth from this book. I pray that it has drawn you closer to the Lover of your soul. But more than anything I pray that these words have brought freedom and assurance that Jesus desires you, loves you, and is faithful because that is who he is.

No more striving.

No more faking.

Just be you with God and everyone else. You are unique, yet so similar to the rest of us.

Her name was Mary, but her name could have been yours. You are being called by the Most High to join his ministry team. Come doubting and fearful, defiant or bitter, come confused and rejected. It doesn't matter what you're like when you come. He's chosen you.

The rest of the story is up to him.

## Journal Opportunity

Write a prayer to God. Give him your praise and thanks. Confess your doubt or bitterness, fear or unbelief. Ask him to fill you with more of his Spirit and to grant you his favor to fulfill the call he has placed on your life. The call does not have to be big. It might be to walk across to your neighbor's house to invite her over for coffee. Don't dismiss the small things. Journal what you hear him telling you. He is faithful.

## Discussion Questions

1. How did Jesus reveal his faithfulness to Mary of Nazareth, his mother? How did God reveal his faithfulness to her?

2. How did Jesus demonstrate his faithfulness to Mary of Bethany?

3. How was Jesus faithful to Mary Magdalene?

4. How has Jesus been faithful to you in your life?

5. What holds you back from moving forward in the calling or ministry you desire to do for the Lord?

6. Is the knowledge that Jesus's faithfulness is not based on our faith encouraging? In what area of your life do you need to incorporate this truth? Does it free you to serve?

# Hearing the Call
## Buried Dreams Bloom

CHAPTER TWELVE COULD NOT BE THE LAST CHAPTER. I WANTED IT TO BE; I LIKE MY LAST sentence. But how could I write a book purposed to encourage women to step into their dreams and callings when I know that many of us can't remember our dreams? Many women have never considered a *call* from God. So, Chapter Thirteen was destined.

## The need to dream

I was in my late twenties when I realized I couldn't remember any dreams for my life. I was so young. It didn't take long for marriage and children—stuff dreams are made of—to overtake me. I know this happens to many of us. Maybe God allows this so that our focus will be on runny noses and little chubby feet rather than our personal pursuits.

But, as I shared in the first chapter, the realization that I couldn't remember my dreams filled me with grief and guilt. I couldn't control my sorrow although my blessings should have filled in the holes. My depression seemed incredibly selfish and sinful.

As Christian women, we're supposed to be joyful and content. Right? The Bible tells us that godliness with contentment is great gain (1 Tim. 6:6). So, when my blessings no longer filled me, and restlessness took up residence, I felt like I was a failing Christian and mommy. Yet I realized how important dreams were the instant I couldn't remember any. Something in me longed for a dream.

I believe all of us long for dreams, but life takes over. Before we know it, we're fifty and we can't remember our dreams beyond the daily grind. But we want to do great things. Is that desire wrong? I've had to search my heart about this too.

But, simply defined, dreams are goals that reach beyond what we think we can do. We were made this way. We were made to stretch and grow. Eternity was placed in our hearts when we were created in the image of God. It's his DNA that calls us to more. He's the God who chooses the weak so that his power can work in us. He's the God who rose from the grave, and I believe he wants to resurrect those dead dreams in us.

He has a purpose, many purposes, and dreams for you.

The truth is: all of us held dreams as a child. All of us. But then we grew up. And life happened. Our dreams either got lost in the chaos of life, or somebody told us we could never fulfill them, and after too many closed doors, we buried them deep inside our hearts. But buried dreams are simply planted seeds.

I wish I could take credit for this wonderful truth, but I must give credit to my husband and to a movie we watched a few years ago. While we watched *The Odd Life of Timothy Green*, I could feel grief threaten my calm disposition as the actors aptly portrayed the pain of a couple unable to conceive. My heart broke as they wrote on paper slips each characteristic they dreamed for a child.

They placed the inked dreams in a small cedar box and buried it in their garden. It was their way of moving on.

I blinked away the tears and held down the sobs bubbling out of my chest. "They are burying a dream," I whispered to Mike. A whisper was all I could muster.

"No, they're planting a seed," he countered gently.

My spirit jumped.

Sure, we knew from the preview that a little boy would grow from their garden, but my sweet man's words walked right past the movie and into my heart. *A buried dream is a planted seed.*

The thought of burying a dream seemed almost wrong . . . painfully wrong, until Mike's words changed my perspective. If you've buried a few dreams, I'm excited for you. You've planted seeds that God will grow. But remember, the seed never looks the same once it blooms. It's always more beautiful.

## The difference between a dream and a calling

In fifth grade I dreamed of sending Delynn Dudenhoeffer to the moon—not because I didn't like her; she dreamed of being an astronaut. I didn't desire to venture into outer space, but it sounded really cool to be the scientist who helped others fly there. I loved the stars and science. My teacher, Mr. Quinner, opened up the night sky to my eleven-year-old brain. That's when I fell in love with those twinkly things on black velvet whose mystery beckoned me to something greater. I loved sitting outside with my dad on warm summer nights under a canopy of stars. We'd drink cold glass bottles of Coke and find the constellations. I loved the heavens.

But math wasn't my best subject and the other science classes after fifth grade were focused on the earth rather than space, so my dream waned until it was extinguished completely. I've never ached to have that dream restored. But it was fun to have it while it lasted. Dreams give us joy. Some dreams are easy to dismiss or let fade into oblivion, but when a dream is accompanied with an ache—if a piece of your heart dies when you give it up, I believe it is more than a dream. It is a calling.

Some of us have buried our *callings* because we were told we couldn't do what we believed God called us to. We have questioned whether we heard him correctly, and we concluded that we didn't. We grieved when this happened.

I was grieving on those North Carolina sands twenty years ago. Looking back, I know that the inability to remember dreams fed that grief, but the heart of the matter was much more than dreams; it was a buried calling.

*Callings* manifest differently for each of us. Mine was a picture that flashed in my mind and my spirit simultaneously after a long time in prayer. I still remember the vision as if it were yesterday, though I was a freshmen in college seeking God's direction.

In the vision I stood in front of a wooden altar much like the one in the tiny Methodist church I attended as a little girl. I wore a clergy robe, and I was holding a Bible. No loud voice shook the room, but I immediately I knew that God was calling me into full-time ministry—pastoral ministry.

I called my parents. They weren't as excited as I was. They told me to get a real college degree. I phoned a friend who (I thought) would celebrate my vision, but she asked me what denomination I planned to preach in. I didn't know that women weren't allowed to preach in some churches. It had never crossed my mind or my spiritual radar that the verses in the Bible about women being silent were applied in our modern era. Her reaction surprised me. I thought that if anyone would understand my calling to preach, she would. Those were the first shovels of dirt thrown onto my calling.

Four years later, I found myself teaching middle-school language arts and attending a church that didn't let women do anything in the worship service—anything. I tried to agree with their doctrine. I even appreciated their simplistic interpretation of the Bible—a very simple perspective that didn't allow historical context to blur the black and white. I buried my calling deep and shoveled some more dirt on top for good measure.

But God knew there was something beautiful lying dormant in that seed for twenty years. And he knew that his visions and dreams for me were more wonderful than any I could create. All I needed to do was surrender (plant) the dream and worship.

## Trust, live, and worship

Trust in the LORD and do good;
> dwell in the land and enjoy safe pasture.
Delight yourself in the LORD,
> and he will give you the desires of your heart.
> (Ps. 37:3–4)

These two verses became my marching orders during those years when dreams went stealth and my calling seemed a figment of my imagination. I was a stay-at-home mom who missed working, and I was a military wife, often a single parent because of my husband's training and deployments. Hard days.

Though I knew God had gifted our family with the financial ability for me stay home with my two little bundles of . . . joy, after three years as a full-time mommy I justified going back to work—only teaching in a private school. I theorized that a private Christian school would be less stressful.

Have you justified your disobedience or bartered with God? If you have, I'm sure you learned as I did that he is in control and wiser. Every job opportunity slipped through my fingers. I was destined to stay home.

Disclaimer: I don't want you to think I believe all moms must stay home with their babies. It was simply what I knew God wanted for me. Honestly, I don't think it was only for my children's sake. They might have been better off at day care. But those hard days taught this soldier of God (me) deep faith lessons.

Hard days come in all shapes and sizes. A difficult job. A loss of a loved one. Illness. A move. Loneliness. Heartbreak. Singleness. Infertility. Anxiety. Financial struggle. Divorce. The list goes on and on. Sometimes our own actions place us in those difficult days; they are the aftermath of our free will. Sometimes they are totally out of our control. But God never intends for these hard days to become our identity or steal our dreams. He can use them to call us to new dreams as well as to resurrect old ones.

## Trusting God

Trust is a four-letter word to some people. They've been hurt by those they trusted, and so this verb got a bad rap. Its reputation got marred by humans. But the psalmist in Psalm 37 gives us the key to living a peaceful life, and it became my first step to finding my dreams again. He tells us to *trust God.*

When the teaching jobs I so desperately wanted fell through, I was distraught. At the time the kids and I were at my parents' for an extended stay while Mike attended a three-month school for officers. My dad, the same one with whom I loved to drink Cokes and stargaze, saw my desperation and fear after I received the notice that I didn't get the job I wanted.

"Where's your faith?" he demanded.

Considering that he wasn't a Christian, his question punched me in the stomach.

Where was my faith?

I had faith that God was in control of the situation. I had faith he didn't want me to work outside my home. But I also believed that I would be lonely and empty for another year or forty years . . . however long God wanted me to be miserable. I did not trust that God had better plans—plans that involved blessings and spiritual growth that I would not have experienced if life had gone my way.

Trusting God starts with the prayer, "Help!"

"Help me trust you, Jesus. Amen."

It's one of the most important prayers we can pray except for this one: "Help me know you love me. Please move that knowledge from my head to my heart."

The people we trust most are those we know love us. But human love, no matter how trustworthy, pales in comparison to God's. God's love—the deep revelation of his love—breathes peace, contentment, joy, and greater measures of faith into our hearts.

He's a good God.

That's where our faith must rest . . . in his goodness.

"'For I know what plans I have in mind for you,' says ADONAI, 'plans for well-being, not for bad things; so that you can have hope and a future'" (Jer. 29:11 CJB).

Trusting God doesn't happen overnight. It doesn't mean you will get everything you ask for in prayer. Trusting God is a lifelong journey, but trusting him was the first step to rediscovering the dreams buried deep inside.

## Do Good

It's God's heart. It is who he is. A God of kindness and mercy, compassion and love in action. And a God who very wisely calls us to do the same. "Trust in the LORD and *do good*" (Ps. 37:3).

Before I jump to what seems obvious, let's dig to find out what David, who wrote Psalm 37, intended by the words "do good." Was he encouraging living a philanthropic life or a life of obedience to God's commands in contrast to the "evil men" in Psalm 37:1 who "do wrong"?

The definitions of the Hebrew words hold treasures that go beyond what our English words translate, and they clarify possible discrepancies in the meaning of this command, *do good.*

"Do" is translated from *'āśāh* (ä-säh). Its definition in the *Key Word* states: "to do, make, work, create, accomplish. . . . Essentially signifies to do or make in a general sense."[1]

Create.

Accomplish.

These words clarify the meaning. Simply obeying laws can qualify as "doing good," but *creating* or *accomplishing* good demands exerting effort for the good of someone else.

"Good" is our English counterpart for the Hebrew word *tôb* (tōve). In Ecclesiastes this word is used "in the context of seeking for the ultimate purpose in life."[2] Granted, Solomon is bemoaning that life seems purposeless, and concludes it is best if a man enjoys his work and eats, drinks, and is merry. But don't miss that the word *tôb* is used in the context of life's *purpose.* In his conclusion Solomon writes: "God will bring every deed into judgment, including every hidden thing, whether it is good or evil" (Eccl. 12:14).

Every. Good. Deed.

Do good, my friends.

In the process of trusting God, waiting on him to reveal his calling and our forgotten dreams, he gives us eternal purpose for each day. Do good. Bless somebody. Invite your neighbor for coffee. Donate to the local homeless shelter. Call a friend who is lonely. Visit your elderly shut-in neighbor. The list is endless.

## Dwell in the land

We moved often as a military family. In our second year of marriage, we moved from Texas to Augusta, Georgia. We lived there only six months, but it seemed like three years. That was my fault. I chose not to get involved in the church or community because we weren't going to be there long.

I was miserable. It didn't help that my baby girl was fussy, Mike studied all the time, and all the women I'd met at church worked, leaving me home all day without friends. But the culprit to my unhappiness wasn't Augusta; it was my decision not to *live* in Augusta. I was surviving. But not living.

The Complete Jewish Bible translates the second half of Psalm 37:3 as "settle in the land."

To *settle* means to make it your home. Set up camp. Stay awhile. Grow roots.

I did hang pictures on the walls of our apartment—that was my idea of *settling*. But if I had chosen to teach Sunday school or volunteer somewhere rather than spend my days decorating, my walls might have been blank, but my heart would have been full. I would have met more people, made a difference in that place, and lived with purpose beyond my life.

After that experience, I vowed to always get involved in our church and community no matter how long the military assignment.

"Settle in the land and feed on faithfulness" (Ps. 37:3b CJB).

I experienced his faithfulness as the years wore on, and I *settled*, not only in the physical places we moved, but in the season of my life as a full-time mom. God was faithful. I wasn't miserable forever. He gave me friends who were also stay-at-home moms. Prayer partners, walking buddies, Bible study groups, and opportunities to teach young girls in our church. The desire for another baby—which was out of the question a few years before—also began to warm my heart. The night we decided to try for a third child, we succeeded. I think God wanted to make it obvious that this nudge, this blessing was from him. As a young girl, I always dreamed of having three children. This buried dream began to bloom.

## Delight in the Lord

"Delight in the LORD, and he will give you the desires of your heart" (Ps. 37:4 NIV). What a wonderful Scripture. It's been on my favorite list for a long time. Such promise—dreams resurrected and callings fulfilled. But before God can give us our heart's desires, we must desire him and enjoy his presence.

For many years I interpreted this word "delight" as worship. When I was in college, I attended a revival in the little pink brick church where I was the youth pastor. Two women played guitars and led the congregants in rousing worship. They lifted their hands, played tambourines, and preached about praising God every hour of the day whether you felt like it or not. This was revolutionary! So, I tried it. And it changed my life. Intentional worship.

I became a praise junkie. There were no Christian music radio stations, so I played my tapes constantly. Twila Paris and Steven Curtis Chapman filled my house and my heart throughout the day. I would make myself sing out loud, and I would dance in my kitchen. I loved to worship Jesus that way. And the more I worshiped him, the more I found myself *delighting* in him.

Synonyms for "delight" are pleasure, happiness, joy, and glee. So, to delight in the Lord is to find our pleasure, happiness, and joy in God.

Which comes first? Worship or delight? I'm not sure it matters. I only know that you really can't have one without the other. And in my life, intentional worship became the core of my heart change.

Intentional worship was fueled by thankfulness too. It didn't always involve music and singing. Many days, when gray clouds hovered in my heart, simply taking a walk helped. I would thank God for the trees or the birds or a flower on the playground behind our house. Thankfulness is magical.

One day as I struggled with Mike's job as a soldier, which kept him too busy and often away from us, the Lord whispered, "Think of all the jobs you're glad he doesn't do, and thank me."

It worked.

As I worshiped and fell in love with the goodness of God, I began to enjoy my life more—even appreciate it. And the old dreams erased by time slowly came back to memory and took breath.

## Dreams for a season

I wouldn't be honest if I told you that life was bliss once I began to trust God, do good, really live wherever we moved, and delighted in him through worship. Bad days sneaked in once in a while. Friends moved or we did, leaving gaps in my heart until new friends were found. Mike's job required almost all of him except on the weekends, though sometimes even the weekends were spent without him—even whole seasons when deployment called.

But God was faithful.

Through the years he unearthed dreams, big and small, and I learned that dreams don't have to be big to be important and life-giving. We all desire God-sized dreams; we were made for that. But I learned I would miss eternal opportunities—the ones that store up treasures in heaven—if I only had my eye on the big dream rather than the small ones unfolding right in front of my face. God has *many* dreams and purposes for us—not just one giant dream, and most of our dreams are only for a season.

One summer when we were stationed in Germany, Mike deployed on a peace-keeping mission to Kosovo. I had recently accepted a leadership role in a chapel women's ministry and was in charge of Bible studies. Though the ministry usually took a break in the summer, I wanted to provide a day of fellowship for all of us who were missing our men. So, I decided to teach an aerobics class once a week. I had participated in a lot of aerobics classes, but I'd never taught one.

Nine-year-old Lauren gathered the most upbeat Christian music we could find at the time (which was sparse). She made a music tape for us, and I memorized a Kathy Ireland routine. Just one.

We did that same routine every week for two months. And we had a blast.

One day after class God whispered in my ear, "You dreamed of being an aerobics instructor . . . remember?"

I left the chapel that day knowing God was on a roll. Slowly but surely he was recovering my dreams and giving me the pleasure of living them. I wasn't a certified instructor but, quite honestly, leading that one class was all I needed. No ache lingered when our sessions ended. A dream had been lived, and it was time to discover the next one.

A few years later we moved back to the States, and God opened doors for my heart dream, my *calling* to preach and teach. The small Nazarene church outside Boston welcomed women in ministry. I soon joined their pastoral staff along with other congregants who felt God's call. And I began taking ministerial classes. I loved almost every minute of it—there were days harder than others. I sailed through classes and clicked through the ordination requirements with speed. I even had the pleasure of preaching a few times, bringing the Bible to life to a group of spiritually hungry people. My biggest fan was my husband.

After each sermon he'd wrap his arm around me and say, "Home run. You hit it out of the park every time."

But something in me knew this dream wouldn't last, and it didn't. Theological differences rose, closing doors for ordination. God's timing was perfect, however, and we moved one more time . . . back to North Carolina.

Those first months after the move I sat in silence, grieving over the closed doors for ordination but thankful that I had lived my dream for a little while. I had tasted it. And that's when I realized that dreams are often for a season. They give us purpose and joy for that season in our life, and then the chapter ends.

But just as that season of ministry ended, a new dream formed inside my heart. You are holding it right now.

Honestly, the dream to write a book seemed too big. But my doubt didn't stop God.

My friends, he is faithful. He made you and me with our quirky personalities, grit, and grace for purposes beyond our imaginations. There are dreams inside you yet to be uncovered, watered, and fed. Be patient. If your dreams are silent, if the call hasn't come . . . wait on him. Make Psalm 37:3–4 your mantra and mode of operation. In the meantime, even if you don't have it all figured out, join the Marys.

You know you fit right in.

*a Mary like Me*

## Notes

[1] Spiros Zodhiates, ed., *The Hebrew-Original Key Word Study Bible, New International Version* (Chattanooga: AMG, 1996), 1542.

[2] Ibid., 1519.

Appendix A

# Resources for Deeper Bible Study

DON'T LIKE DEBATES AND HATE CONFRONTATION. BUT AFTER YEARS OF ATTENDING DIFFERENT churches and studying diverse Bible translations, I started asking questions. Why does one denomination believe *this* and another denomination believe *that* based on the same Bible? Why does one Scripture translation use this English word and another use a different word?

These questions made me question religious doctrine and tradition. Suddenly I—despite an initial fear of people—desired to go beyond convention. I realized that nobody has "arrived." No translation can claim perfection; no denomination has gleaned all the correct answers (though some think they have, and some are definitely closer than others). We are all on a journey to find truth.

I like to question tradition. This has gotten me into trouble, but it has also opened up a whole new understanding of the Bible for me. The Scriptures have come to life because I have not settled for conventional commentaries as my only source of study. This is where the Marys come into play. Much of what we believe about these biblical women is due to tradition. To be painfully honest, much of what we believe about them is based on commentaries written by men—not women.

All commentators (including me) wear their own filters as they study the Bible. These filters include gender, economic status, our childhood experience or traumas, and our health. Our experiences and personalities affect how we read our Bibles. This is called a "hermeneutical bias." These are big words that simply mean "nobody is perfect." A translation or commentary is written on the basis of the commentator's own experience with God and man.

Whether you are Catholic or Protestant, denominational or non-denominational, your beliefs have been affected by religious tradition too. You may want to argue with me concerning this; however, it's our human nature to pass down our beliefs and faith through established teaching. There are many things we believe because of a song we've sung, a ritual we've performed, a movie we've watched, or a sermon we've heard. That is why we must read and study the Bible on our own as well as in corporate worship.

The final component that affects the translation of Bibles is language. Years ago a Beth Moore Bible study inspired me to search for Hebrew and Greek words in Scriptures. It was revelatory to me. I had never considered studying this way. Though I knew the Bible was translated from ancient languages, I didn't realize how this could affect the meaning. Yet as I studied, I realized that a word in one language does not always have a perfect counterpart in the translated language. Translators have done their best, but because the English doesn't hold a perfect counterpart, unique aspects of the ancient words are lost in our modern language.

A friend knew of my intrigue with the language and introduced me to the *Key Word Study Bible*. This resource was life-changing in my walk with the Lord and my study of Scripture. (Thank you, Bonnie!) The *Key Word* contains bold numbers printed next to specific words. Old Testament and New Testament dictionaries in the back of the book provide the corresponding Hebrew or Greek definitions annotated by the editor, Dr. Spiros Zodhiates, the originator of this study Bible.

The *Key Word* was published by AMG Publishers based on their main goal: "to make key aspects of the vocabulary and syntax of the original languages *available and understandable for everyone, whether or not they had formal training in the biblical languages.*"[1] I believe AMG has succeeded, and I'm eternally grateful for their goal and their labor. I can't adequately stress the value of this resource. I believe in this resource so much that I give these books away periodically on my website, wordsbyandylee.com.

In each chapter of *A Mary like Me* I have highlighted ancient words from a Scripture passage. I've tried to stay away from the term "original" when referring to those Hebrew and Greek words because there is much debate on whether the original manuscripts of the New Testament—especially the Gospels, were written in Hebrew, Aramaic, or Greek. The New Testament in our Bibles was translated from Greek transcripts.

It's possible that the Gospels were written in Hebrew or Aramaic before being translated into Greek, but finding the Greek word that was translated into our English language allows us to hear the Scripture in a historical language one step closer, if you will, to the Hebrew or Aramaic manuscripts. This often reveals a different possible reading of the Scripture at hand and gives new insight to its meaning beyond customary commentary.

My sources for the Hebrew and Greek text include *The Key Word Study Bible* and online sources. There are several trustworthy online sources, but the one I recommend is blueletterBible.org. The interlinear tool on this site gives the Hebrew and Greek words from the selected text, along with their definitions and common uses.

It's my hope that the insight I've received from my study will encourage you and empower you to begin your own research. These sources I've suggested will assist you to go beyond the traditional teachings as the Spirit leads. As you begin to research, however, always consider the context of the Scripture, the culture of the time period, particularly the Hebrew culture, and how the words you're studying are used in other Scriptures. This will help you to maintain the entire biblical perspective as you ponder a specific text.

We are living in a time like no other for serious students of the Bible. We have many resources at our fingertips that were at one time only available for Bible scholars in seminaries. Don't wait for someone to feed you; begin your own excavation. The Word of God will come to life.

## Note

[1]Spiros Zodhiates, ed., *The Hebrew-Original Key Word Study Bible, New International Version* (Chattanooga: AMG Publishers, 1996), preface.

# Intercessory Wisdom for Ministry

M ENTAL ILLNESS AND DEPRESSION ARE SERIOUS PROBLEMS IN OUR WORLD TODAY, AND they seem to be growing. Here are some key concepts for intercessory deliverance ministry. Based on the Word of God:

**1. As the Israelites painted their door frames with the blood of the lamb, we must put on the armor of God before going into battle and pray for the blood of Christ to cover us. This is war.**

Paul's words help us understand the battle and prepare for it. He is very clear:

> Put on the full armor of God so that you can take your stand against the devil's schemes. For our struggle is not against flesh and blood, but against the rulers, against the authorities, against the powers of this dark world and against the spiritual forces of evil in the heavenly realms. Therefore put on the full armor of God, so that

> when the day of evil comes, you may be able to stand
> your ground, and after you have done everything, to
> stand. Stand firm then, with the belt of truth buckled
> around your waist, with the breastplate of righteousness
> in place, and with your feet fitted with the readiness
> that comes from the gospel of peace. In addition to all
> this, take up the shield of faith, with which you can
> extinguish all the flaming arrows of the evil one. Take
> the helmet of salvation and the *sword of the Spirit, which
> is the word of God* . . . and pray. (Eph. 6:11–18a, empha-
> sis mine)

Putting on our spiritual armor and praying for the blood of Jesus
to cover us are two important aspects of our defense against the
enemy, but we must not forget God's powerful offensive weapon—
his Word. I find it powerful and important to pray Scripture. I often
pray with my Bible open, aware of the Holy Spirit's leading. I might
open to a psalm and begin reading it and praying it. The Scriptures
are the sword of the Spirit. We must do battle with God's truth.

**2. Every demonic spirit that is cast out or bound must be replaced
with a godly spirit.**

As I pray to cast out a demonic spirit, I pray for Christ to replace
it with the Holy Spirit. In place of anger and bitterness, I ask that
Christ give his Spirit of wisdom, knowledge, grace, and peace.
Listen to Jesus's warning:

> When an impure spirit comes out of a person, it goes
> through arid places seeking rest and does not find it.
> Then it says, "I will return to the house I left." When it
> arrives, it finds the house swept clean and put in order.

Then it goes and takes seven other spirits more wicked than itself, and they go in and live there. And the final condition of that person is worse than the first. (Luke 11:24–26 NIV)

**3. This kind of ministry can only be done through prayer and fasting.**

Jesus told this to his disciples after they couldn't heal a boy with an evil spirit, "This kind can come out only by prayer" (Mark 9:29). Personally, I've found I need at least one other person (if not a team of people) praying and fasting with me. When I struggle in fasting, I know the battle is great. But when I'm not alone in the fight, camaraderie with fellow soldiers gives me inspiration to complete the fast.

**4. The person must desire to be free.**

I think this is the hardest lesson I've learned. We can know all of the correct Scriptures to pray. We can know what spirits to bind and loose. But if the people to whom we're desperately ministering don't want to change, if they only want Jesus to change their lives but not their hearts and minds, all the binding and loosing in the world will not bring freedom. Our God has given us free will, and he will not go beyond the boundaries he has put in place. So I'm learning to pray for people to recognize their need for change, their need for deliverance, their need for Jesus. With great wisdom in this area of ministry, Francis Frangipane writes:

> Deliverance is often just that simple when a soul is willing. Yet, without some measure of repentance, deliverance is almost always impossible, for although a spirit may be commanded to leave, if the structure of the

individual's thoughts has not been changed, his wrong attitude toward sin will welcome that spirit back.[1]

Frangipane's book, *The Three Battlegrounds,* is an excellent source I recommend to all involved in ministry and intercession.

## Note

[1]Francis Frangipane, *The Three Battlegrounds* (Cedar Rapids: Arrow Publications, 1989), 27.

# Instructions for *Mary Group* Leaders

F IRST, MAY I TELL YOU HOW PROUD I AM OF YOU? YOU ARE STEPPING OUT IN FAITH. SOME of you may be seasoned leaders who will not need this encouragement and instruction, but some of you may be brand new at this. Thank you for becoming a leader of a *Mary Group.*

It may seem strange to have an odd number of chapters, but this allows you to have an introductory session where you can distribute the books, get to know each other better, and discuss what each one of you hopes to glean from the book and your time together. The short chapters and limited discussion questions make it possible to double the chapters per week, crafting your group as a seven-week study. It's up to you and the consensus of the group. However, one of my *Mary Groups* complained when we doubled up on the chapters each week. They preferred one chapter at a time.

We are an extremely busy society. Most women wear many hats, so find what works for you, and remember to extend much grace to yourself as the leader as well as to your group members. I know each *Mary Group* will have its own flavor and flair, but there are a few things that are essential to every group and every meeting:

## Prayer

Please begin praying for your group before you advertise or invite people. And after the group has formed, pray for the members daily. One of my favorite activities to encourage prayer for one another is to have each member write a prayer request, fold it, and place it in a basket. After everyone has placed their request in the basket, take turns drawing out a request. Each person then prays daily for that request. It is good to do this every week. Our hearts are drawn together as we pray for one another.

## Laughter

It is my prayer that the *Mary Groups* laugh together. Start the first few meetings with icebreakers. One of the easiest is the M&M "get to know you" game. Instruct the women to take some M&M's but not eat them. After everyone has gotten a handful, tell them that you are going to share facts about yourselves. They are to share one fact per candy. This is not Nazi M&M's. If someone has grabbed a couple of handfuls, don't force her to share for every single one. Remember, grace abounds in these groups. This game can also be played with toilet paper. For every square of paper taken, facts are shared. But personally, I think chocolate is a lot more fun.

Sometimes I open new groups with instruction for each person to share three facts about themselves and what they had for breakfast that morning or the color of their toothbrush. These are random questions. But the answers are often funny and very telling of the person's personality. Have fun with it. Ask the Lord to help you love the women he puts in this group. Ask him to bring joy and laughter into your group.

## Worship

Worship of Jesus is demonstrated in many ways. We can worship him with music, in prayer, in confession of his power in our lives, and by reading of his Word out loud. We worship him when we lay our burdens and fears at his feet. Spend time worshiping the Lord together during your group meetings. I suggest that after you have an icebreaker or some "get to know each other" time, spend time in worship before you delve into the questions. Here are some suggestions:

- Play a contemporary worship song. No one has to sing, just close your eyes and worship together.
- Distribute Bible verses to group members that give praise to God and his wonderful attributes. Pray as a group, turning those Scriptures into praise. Each woman takes a turn to pray her assigned Scripture.
- Pray the ABC's. I love this prayer. Pray using the ABC's to guide you through God's attributes. For example: "God, I praise you. You are the only one to be Adored! I praise you because you are Beautiful and Compassionate . . ."
- Take time to give praise for answered prayers and God's hand in our lives.
- If you have a member who sings or plays an instrument, paints, or writes, invite her to bless the group with her praise to Jesus, using her talent.

## Prayer

Yes, I have already written about the importance of prayer. But I want to reiterate it. Open in prayer. Pray as needs arise in your discussions of the chapters. And close in prayer.

I will be praying for you.

Remember . . . *nothing is impossible with God.*